vanquishing
ghosts
and
demons

About the Author

Sandrea Mosses (Staffordshire, UK) was trained as a medium with the Spiritual National Union and has worked as a professional medium for more than fifteen years. She specializes in the art of banishments and clearings. From the beginning, her spirit guides have assisted her in safely removing ghouls, demons, and other dark entities from our world.

To Write the Author

If you wish to contact the author or would like more information about this book, please write to the author in care of Llewellyn Worldwide, and we will forward your request. Both the author and publisher appreciate hearing from you and learning of your enjoyment of this book and how it has helped you. Llewellyn Worldwide cannot guarantee that every letter written to the author can be answered, but all will be forwarded. Please write to:

Sandrea Mosses
℅ Llewellyn Worldwide
2143 Wooddale Drive
Woodbury, MN 55125-2989

Please enclose a self-addressed stamped envelope for reply, or $1.00 to cover costs. If outside the USA, enclose an international postal reply coupon.

SANDREA MOSSES

vanquishing
ghosts
and
demons

....

A Medium's Harrowing Tales
of Removing Evil Spirits

Llewellyn Publications
Woodbury, Minnesota

FIRST EDITION
First Printing, 2014

Book design by Bob Gaul
Cover design by Kevin R. Brown
Cover images: iStockphoto.com/18191178/©Yaroslav Gerzhedovich
        iStockphoto.com/15218300/©Boris Rabtsevich
        iStockphoto.com/3232769/©Lou Oates
Editing by Patti Frazee
Interior border art: "Decorative French Ironwork Designs CD-ROM
        and Book," © 2006 by Dover Publications, Inc.

Llewellyn Publications is a registered trademark of Llewellyn Worldwide Ltd.

Library of Congress Cataloging-in-Publication Data
Mosses, Sandrea.
  Vanquishing ghosts & demons: a medium's harrowing tales of removing
evil spirits/Sandrea Mosses.—First Edition.
     pages cm
  ISBN 978-0-7387-3645-7
1. Exorcism. 2. Demonology. 3. Occult sciences. I. Title. II. Title:
Vanquishing ghosts and demons.
  BF1559.M67 2014
  133.4'27—dc23
                        2014011643

Llewellyn Publications does not participate in, endorse, or have any authority or responsibility concerning private business transactions between our authors and the public.
  All mail addressed to the author is forwarded, but the publisher cannot, unless specifically instructed by the author, give out an address or phone number.
  Any Internet references contained in this work are current at publication time, but the publisher cannot guarantee that a specific location will continue to be maintained. Please refer to the publisher's website for links to authors' websites and other sources. Cover model(s) used for illustrative purposes only and may not endorse or represent the book's subject.

Llewellyn Publications
A Division of Llewellyn Worldwide Ltd.
2143 Wooddale Drive
Woodbury, MN 55125-2989
www.llewellyn.com

Printed in the United States of America

CONTENTS

Acknowledgments

Bill: Anonymous

Bev: A proficient psychic and energy worker

Karen: A talented medium

Kevin: A naturally gifted medium with
strong shamanic connections

Lyn: Gifted medium, Angelic Reiki Master, a
powerful energy worker, and a key team member

Linda: Brilliant medium and teacher

Martin: Gifted spiritual and
Reiki healer, animal healer, and psychic

Paul: Anonymous, but one
of the key team members

Patrick: A talented light worker,
Reiki Master, and psychic

Rachel: Adept psychic and Reiki Master

Marilou Trask-Curtin: Author/screenwriter/
playwright for her help with this book

*Even though the names in this book are changed,
I would like to thank all those who placed their
faith and trust in me and the team to help clear
their properties of unwanted entities.*

DEDICATION

To all my team members for their dedication; Cherry for my journey; Stella for her inspiration; my family for sharing me; Lyn for looking after me; and David for being you and always being there for me.

Introduction

Within our world there exists another world—a world of ghosts, ghouls, and demons that have the capabilities of silently entering lives and wreaking havoc. Most of the time these beings are unheard and unseen until it is too late. I have dedicated my life to fighting these disembodied fiends.

I never intended to become a ghost hunter, but a terrifying incident in my teens sparked a fascination with the paranormal. I am a medium who is both clairvoyant and clairsentient. This means I can see spirits, ghosts, and demons and, even when they try to hide from me, I can sense their presence. I developed my psychic skills many years ago and became extremely well-read and well-trained in all aspects of the paranormal. The gifts I possess enable me to see beyond this world and into the spirit world; I can communicate with entities through the spoken word and with my mind.

I sometimes come in contact with demons. Many of these demons have powers far greater than my team or I could ever imagine. A good team is comprised of many different talents and skill levels. I'm fortunate to work with other psychics and mediums, energy workers, Reiki Masters, healers, and light workers. Each story in this book will introduce you to these talented people who work beside me.

Thankfully, there is also help from the other side in the form of spirit guides. Without the assistance of our guides we would never be able to overcome these evil entities. My personal spirit guides are Quan Yin, White Feather, White Cloud, and Saul.

Quan Yin (sometimes spelled Kuan Yin) is a Chinese deity. She is a goddess of compassion and suffering and she hears the cries of the world. She always appears to me as a great beauty. Her dark hair is set in a bun on the top of her head, like a crown. A veil covers the bun and cascades down her back and front; it does not cover her face. Her skin is very pale and almost translucent. She wears a white robe that flows as she moves.

White Feather is well over six feet tall and is a white, shimmering being with long silver hair. When White Feather presents himself to me he is always dressed in a long, flowing cape made up of hundreds of small white feathers. When he is assisting me in a clearance I will see his feathers sweep through the victim as he attempts to knock an entity off a person.

White Cloud is a Native American who is strong and incredibly powerful. He protects and gives me psychic power to use against demonic forces.

Saul is an ancient being who resided on earth thousands of years ago. He rarely presents himself to me, but when he does, he appears as medium height, very old, and very wise. He has gray hair and a closely trimmed beard. He is usually dressed in a sapphire blue robe. Saul guides me through the clearance as he mentally communicates to me what skills to use during the different encounters. Saul also shows me where to look for the entities when they are trying to hide.

The majority of the time my communication with my guides is psychic. Images and voices will come into my mind; it's almost like looking at a television screen. There are times when I am in extreme danger that I will psychically see the demonic forces I am fighting. The other side will illuminate the predator for us when either I or one of my teammates are about to be in jeopardy so we can see what the demon is trying to do.

One of the most difficult clearings my team and I have come across was with the demon Jezabeth; I admit I have never encountered power like hers before. There seemed to be nothing outside her capabilities, but what made her more dangerous was the way she counter-attacked. Jezabeth was always attacking as many people in the group as she could at one time. Jezabeth also used other means to confuse and distract, such as sounds—banging, tapping, and moving things. She understood the psyche of the human mind and she used it to her advantage. Every encounter my team and I had with her always took us to the edge of our abilities. Through it all, this evil entity remained totally unfazed by everything we were doing as she toyed with us.

This book is about my experiences as a psychic: clearing demons, darkness, disembodied entities, and the battles that have ensued. Within these pages is a chronicle of my encounters with the dark, supernatural forces of evil as I pitched my psychic gifts against the powers of darkness. You will read of times when I almost lost the fight and found myself in their evil grasp as they tried to possess me, and times when I was at my most vulnerable or asleep and the demons have returned and tried to attack me.

I still vividly recall the first time that happened, and I was caught off guard. The clearance was reaching its final stages when from the back of the human victim rose a winged creature. The entity had a birdlike head with amber eyes that scanned the room with menace in its steely, cold gaze. This demon grew from nothing to a fiend with a three-foot wingspan. Intentionally it stretched its clawed foot towards me and psychically pierced my stomach as it forced its claw into me, wrapped itself around me like a shawl, and disappeared into my soul. Without the skill of my guides on the other side and the friends who were assisting me, I, too, would have easily been the next victim.

One

Understanding How We Work

Every profession has its own terminology and its own rules, and my team is no different. Some of our methods will run contrary to what is usually thought to be the norm for ghost hunting, but one thing is certain: when we are on an investigation we work as one and always watch each other's backs—because it can be no other way when we're up against the demonic.

When a call for help comes in I rarely tell the other team members about the full extent of the disturbance prior to going to the property and, in fact, they are given the least amount of information possible. The reason for this is relatively simple—anything they perceive is not going to be tainted by any prior knowledge. Also, we are not a group that is interested in scientifically proving or disproving anything—our full intent and focus is in determining what, if anything is in the house or on the property and then dealing with it by utilizing our own methods. When the group is able to either verify or discount the occupant's interpretation of events, we are halfway to success.

I always meet with the team beforehand and we spend time harmonizing our energies so that we are able to function as one. During this initial meeting we also take the opportunity to clarify our roles for the time ahead.

When our team carries out a rescue or banishment we have with us a healer who is there to offer help to both the victims and the perpetrators. The healer is able to see damage to the auric field, repair it, and utilize the healing vibration to help the lost soul or souls on the journey to their particular home. Also with us on a call are at least three strong mediums that provide the power to move the entities from one world to another jointly with the other side. It must be stated that when we are dealing with a demon, it takes a colossal amount of combined energy to facilitate the shift. Any mediums present cannot be frightened or swayed by anything thrown at them—even a personal attack. Believe me, we have sometimes barely managed to overcome a demon even with four of us working in unison!

After arriving at the site, one of the first things we do is to determine what, if anything, is in or on the property, because we need to know exactly what we are dealing with—be it a demon or simply a lost soul—both of which require different levels of energy to facilitate a "pass over," a crossing over to the other side. Please understand that whatever entity is present is not likely to want to move on and will go to great lengths to avoid detection.

Once we establish what we are dealing with, we then psychically seal the property in sheafs of light so we can contain the entity. Sheafs of light is a powerful visualization technique that utilizes colors—each color vibrating differently—to create boundaries that disembodied spirits cannot traverse. The entire property, including the roof, floors, and adjoining walls of any buildings are encased in the sheafs of light. By doing this we ensure that any entities in or on the property are contained and cannot hide from us or escape.

Throughout the clearance we will continue to use a variety of different tools or techniques—both physical and mental. Sometimes we make use of crystals to intensify and increase the power needed. The type of crystal will depend on what we are trying to achieve. We also use "points," which is a method that allows us to focus energy on a precise point. Spheres are a method used to mentally scatter power across a room, thus creating small tornadoes of energy to cleanse and replenish the power in that space. Mexican waves remove residue of dark vibrations left behind from a recent trauma. Walls of light are used to redirect ley (energy) lines and to cleanse the ether.

Together the team decides where to open a "doorway." This is the means by which spirits cross over. After we decide where to place the doorway, we then do a visualization and open the doorway using silver light.

After the space is cleared, we use concentrated blocks of visualized color to seal doorways and portals to other worlds. In the end, it is the joining of our vibrations via any of these techniques that magnifies our earthly power and removes stubborn and destructive forces from the site.

One of the greatest gifts of all in our arsenal is the joining of the two worlds—earth and the other side—through communication with our spirit guides (and everyone in the group has their own special guides). My main guide is White Feather, a force who oversees all of these clearings. We are equally blessed to have one another, as without us the other side cannot effectively remove these entities and vice versa.

Please understand then that my team and I are not the ones who perform a clearance—we are merely the link here on earth. Yes, our psychic powers and various vibrational connections with one another are necessary to facilitate the clearance—but essentially we do not take the lost soul, entity, or demon through to the other side. This is the role of those on the other side, such as the guides. The spirit world is a vast place with many dimensions, and we as mortals would not know where to place an entity. For example, to remove a soul and put it in a place with too much light might destroy it. Further, we would not know where a soul came from in that vastness that is the other side. This is why we won't attempt to do a clearance in isolation, but we do it in tandem with the other side.

Thankfully, I must report, we have never suffered from any long-lasting effects because of this work, but each and every one of us have, at some time, suffered from both physical and psychic attacks.

And therein lies the caution.

Before you consider tackling any of the entities described in this book, think very carefully. We are, in effect, the ambassadors of our guides as well as their helpers, and our group is guided every step of the way. Would I attempt to facilitate a clearance without this backup?

Never!

A Bit of History

The term "haunting" has been used to describe a wide variety of unearthly phenomena—from the ethereal scenes of a battle from a long-ago time playing out in the present to the tender sighting of a departed relative watching over a sleeping child. A haunting may also be of a more menacing type—an encounter with a demonic force bent on causing destruction.

Historically, England has been reported to have more than its share of ghosts. One of the most famous alleged hauntings is that of the Bloody Tower of London where the apparitions of two murdered young princes, King Edward V and his younger brother Richard, are often seen. The boys are said to appear in their nightclothes, holding hands, before fading away into the brickwork. There does not appear to be any sort of a pattern to their appearances, but they are seen on a regular basis.

This type of phenomenon has been reported from around the world, particularly from places where a tragic event, such as the murder of the two young princes, has occurred. The horror of the occurrence seems to psychically stain the earth with such force that the event replays itself over and over at key times.

Although not classified as a haunting it bears mentioning that during wartimes there have always been reports from people who see the ghost of a loved one standing at the foot of their bed. Many a mother or wife has been awakened from a sound sleep to clearly see the form of their son or husband standing there and telling the news of their recent death. This is often called a "crisis apparition," as the spirit is anxious to impart the news of their recent passing to their loved ones before beginning their journey home to the afterlife. Oftentimes, this was the only way a family knew the truth of the death.

Another reason for a haunting comes about when someone dies unexpectedly, such as through some sort of accident, and they don't realize they are dead, especially if they did not, during life, consider what awaited them after death. While they could be considered ghosts, they truly do not wish to harm the living—they are merely dead without realizing it and continuing to carry on with their daily routines as though they were still living. They even view their former residences as existing exactly as they did when they were alive, despite the fact that all their belongings have been removed. When new owners take over the house, the spirit views those occupants as squatters and may attempt a variety of disturbances in an effort to get the family to leave. Sometimes, even the house itself is long gone and yet the spirit sees it as still standing whole and as real as it was during the days they lived there in physical form.

Then there are those souls who know they are dead but refuse to move on to the light—they remain here on earth because they fear meeting up with someone on the other side or facing up to something they did while still alive. Our group once dealt with a case in Bridgnorth where we came across the spirit of a man who had accidently killed his father. The father, in a drunken rage, had beaten his son and, in order to protect himself, the son had pushed his father away and killed him in the process. For years after his death, the spirit of the son had hidden in a barn and been afraid to go to the light despite the efforts of the other side to rescue him.

And then there are the hauntings by the true denizens of darkness.

There are those who have lived their lives by harnessing the darkness through violence, drink, drugs, and such. They refuse to go into the light because—even though they are dead—their one desire is to continue their debauchery. These spirits stalk the earth, creating fear and looking for victims to feed off of, enticing them to take substances that destroy them and envelop them in the darkness.

An entity of this sort was known to be in a hotel in the north of England, and this ghost had developed the ability to appear fleetingly in a mirror there. This apparition was enough to terrify an innocent guest at the hotel, thus creating a bolt of fear in the person. The ghost greedily harvested this fear. Some of these types of spirits can, over time, develop the ability to move objects—often described as poltergeist activity—in order to satisfy their greed through fear.

One of the absolute worst types of hauntings is demonic, and they arrive on earth in various ways, most typically through black magic or by being invited here through the use of the Ouija board or other tools of spirit communication. Most of the entities that come through have never lived in our world and have no understanding and no desire whatsoever to comprehend anything about earthly life. They are powerful, ruthless, and without emotion. They are afraid of nothing and no one. They are intelligent, skillful with mind manipulation, and they are the hardest of entities to remove from this world.

———————

The following will give a good illustration of the types of entities we come up against on a regular basis. Here are a few tales of an alcoholic ghost, a shape-shifting demon that turns into a dragon, and more!

It's in My Head

Richard and Eve approached me following a charity event at a local spiritualist center because they had heard through a mutual friend of my ability to cleanse ghosts from properties. In fact, they had attended this event with the sole purpose of seeking me out.

Eve told me that about four years prior, she and her boys had moved into Richard's spacious apartment, which was located in a low-rise block. Things seemed ideal—ideal, that was, until Eve began feeling a little bit uncomfortable when she was home alone. Despite this, Eve didn't immediately notice anything *wrong*, but over time the realization became stronger.

At first, Eve discounted her feelings as paranoia—and these were overwhelming sensations that she was being watched whenever she was alone in the apartment. These feelings of being observed closely were particularly strong in the bathroom and when she was in a state of undress. Eventually, there began to be physical occurrences in the apartment, such as violent banging and shaking of the bedroom door whenever she and Richard tried to be intimate.

Even the children were not spared. Normally the boys rarely argued, but quite suddenly arguments amongst them seemed to occur with increased regularity and, even worse, the boys were being plagued by the appearance of something with red eyes that watched their every move. Soon Richard and Eve found themselves bickering with one another over trivial matters.

At first Richard mocked the idea of someone or something watching Eve, but he could not ignore the violence with which the inside bedroom door seemed to reverberate every time he tried to move close to Eve. By the time our group arrived at the scene, the strain on the faces of both Richard and Eve was clearly visible.

As usual the team first met outside and waited until we were all present before entering the property. My team consisted of Linda, a brilliant medium and teacher, Bill, a medium with strong shamanic connections, and Paul. As a precautionary measure, we sealed not only the apartment but the whole block with sheafs of light in hopes this would prevent whatever was there from moving from one place to another.

I had also given the others only a sliver of data concerning the activity on the property and, despite this, the group was almost immediately able to ascertain that the bedrooms of the apartment were where the energy fluctuation seemed to be the most intense. So these rooms were our natural starting points as they would be in many of the places we investigated—bedrooms were natural hiding places for entities and the room in which we are the most vulnerable to psychic attacks, especially when deeply asleep.

We entered the children's bedroom first. The space was most definitely a boy's room full of war toys, posters, and typical dark and dismal coloring. There were single beds to the left and right of the door and a range of wardrobes and chests of drawers with even more piles of toys.

We formed a circle and brought in Richard and Eve and placed them between us. When everyone was ready, we all began to focus on the room.

Linda started our night's work out quickly. She sensed the spirits of an elderly couple in the corner of the bedroom and her findings were supported by both Bill and Paul. The couple was standing together and the man had a protective arm around his wife's shoulder. Both of them had an air of bewilderment about them.

Something here was not right. I felt sure this was a deception and that the elderly couple were being presented to us as a means of throwing us off the trail of the real culprit. It was almost as if the perpetrator had recently captured the couple and they were being held there in his energy lair waiting for the next group of ghost hunters to come along. This entity, whatever it was, had found a means of remaining aloof and he was going to keep using it to his advantage.

I felt compelled to intervene. "Let's ignore the couple for the moment." I said this because I felt that whatever was causing trouble here was hiding behind the man and woman. "I feel we need to look for something else that is not of this world."

Whatever was here was not going to give up easily and, in fact, I was sure it would use every means it could to avoid detection. I began to scan the room quickly.

"Whatever it is, I feel it is definitely hiding from us," Linda said.

"I agree," Paul said and added, "Sandrea, I'm aware of something underneath the bed and in the far right corner." He pointed to the area concerned. "I feel it's hiding, but I don't think it's afraid of us. It just seems to be trying to avoid us."

We were all in agreement and began to manipulate the energy in the corner to pull this entity—or what we now felt was a demonic force—out from its hiding place. We weaved waves of energy behind the demonic force to flush it away from the wall. As we did so we began to draw it towards us. As soon as we started this process Richard started to complain of a headache. Very much what one would term a "man's man," Richard did not seem the type to complain openly of headache pain. He might only have been 5'8", but this was one powerful guy whose biceps were visible from beneath his shirt. If he was complaining in front of all of us, this must have been bad.

"I feel like I have a tight band around my head," Richard said.

I could see that Richard was beginning to feel more than a little uncomfortable. He wiped at his brow and loosened the collar of his shirt. "It's getting really bad," he said, and then, before anyone could speak, he added, "It really hurts!" His hands immediately flew to his head and he pressed the palms of both hands against his temples. "It hurts! Get it out! Get it out! There's something in my head!"

As Richard spoke, his hands never left his head. His eyes began to bulge as if an extreme force was being applied to his skull. He twisted his head from side to side, making it appear that he was fighting some unseen force.

"Richard!" I yelled. "Look at me!"

"I can't. It's bloody killing me! Help me!"

Richard's whole upper body rotated from side to side. For me, this had gone on long enough. "Richard! Do you hear? Look at me!" This time I commanded him and squeezed his arm to emphasize my point. As soon as our eyes met, the spell the demonic force held over him seemed to be broken. Richard slowly calmed down and the pain and panic he had been experiencing began to subside. He took his hands away from his head and wiped the beads of sweat off his forehead. At the same time, our group member Bill stepped forward. He placed a reassuring hand on Richard and, using Reiki and soothing thoughts, began to minister healing on and around the head area. Slowly Richard began to take control of himself and, as the pain and pressure left his body, the realization of what had just happened became clearer to him. He apologized profusely to the group and we could all see he was very embarrassed by the whole episode.

"Don't worry," I said. "This entity is playing with us. It is using any means it can to delay the inevitable." I paused and looked at Richard. "Are you okay for us to continue?"

"I'm fine. Let's get it over and done with!" He pursed his lips as he spoke, and I could see that he was now angry that this beast had been able to cause him such discomfort. More importantly, I knew, the entity had humiliated him and attacked his masculinity in front of his partner and a group of strangers.

Every one of us was beginning to realize this demon was a more powerful being than we had at first realized. It seemed it had incredible ability to cause pain through mind control, and it reminded me of Azazel, a biblical fallen angel.

With Richard now much calmer, we began to focus fully on what we had in the room with us. And I must remark that all during this diversion with Richard, the other side had intervened and had been busy holding the demon in a box of light from which there was no escape.

We now knew the demon's location and size (about 2'6"), and we were about to begin to move it—although it was now quite obvious to us that this was a shape-shifting entity with the ability to change its form and size almost instantaneously. It was black in color with what can only be described as black dreadlocks from head to foot. At the moment we were looking at it, the entity appeared to be harmless, but we were wise enough not to be fooled. We tried to hold our vibrations in preparation of shifting this *thing* from its present location.

No sooner had we started the process when Eve began to cry. At first there were just small, gentle sobs, and then the crying increased in volume to the point where she was openly sobbing. Linda asked Eve what was wrong. "I feel like I am killing a child—my child," she said while continuing to cry. "It feels so kind, caring, and loving. Almost like a child. It is so sad to be sent from our world. It's asking me to be the mother. It feels like a small, helpless child."

I could not believe the lengths this small demon would go to stay in our dimension—but I knew I shouldn't be surprised. Then, to make matters worse, I found out that Eve and Richard had been trying to have a baby for the past eighteen months. The demon had known this and was using it to manipulate Eve.

Linda took the lead. "Eve, do you remember what this thing has been doing to your boys?" Without waiting for an answer, Linda pressed on. "Haven't both your children been afraid because of this beast? Hasn't it been causing them to argue and fall out with each other?"

In between her sobs, Eve nodded her head in agreement. I could feel that Eve was beginning to remember the impact this demon was having on her boys. She seemed to have a moment of clarity as she remembered what this entity had been doing to each and every one of them. The change could clearly be seen in her stature before she spoke. She physically changed her position, wiped her eyes, and began to stand tall. Eve turned to Linda and said, "Yes, you're right. Please get rid of it! Please make it stop making me feel this way!"

"We will honey," Linda said reassuringly. "Just a little while longer, then it will be over."

For the beast, all hope was now lost. There was no one else for it to influence. Suddenly, this cute little monster turned back to what it truly was—a powerful and malevolent demon—as it began to assume the form of a dragon!

We gave it no chance to pull in its true power. It was well and truly boxed in. I stood back and allowed White Feather to do his work in tandem with his spirit helpers. In just moments, they began the process of dismantling the entity from our universe and returning it to its own dimension. It did not, of course, go easily, and lashed out energetically at us all. We merely batted it back. At the same time we hit it with the worst vibration of all—we sent it love, and then more. This was the only effort required from us to help it on its way and soon it was gone forever. Gone, that is, until such time that someone unwittingly invites it back.

Having removed the demon, we turned our energies to the elderly spirit couple who continued to stand in the corner of the bedroom watching the whole episode in total amazement. These two were clearly frightened by what they had witnessed but appeared none the worse for the experience. They were not lost souls who needed to be rescued—they were souls wandering through who had been, for a short period of time, entangled in the demon's vibration. They were very glad to be released and they simply stepped through the doorway back to their own world.

After the elderly couple had been taken care of, we quickly checked the remaining rooms in the apartment and all appeared free from further intrusion. It is known that ghosts or demons can easily move through building fabrics and are often able to avoid detection because they simply go to an adjacent property. We did take the precaution of extending our energies into the apartments above, below, and to the side and all were clear; however, I was sure Richard and Eve were not the only occupants to be tormented by this entity.

We would never know how this entity had found a doorway into this world, but hopefully it was banished forever.

You Forgot to Ask Permission

I first met Mandy at work. We had quite a good relationship even before someone finally told her of my "hidden talent." When she found out, she inquired if I would look at her house because she felt there was something in the place that was frightening her little girl, Katie.

During our frequent conversations Mandy had said their house was a new-built, which meant that she and her husband Ben had built it themselves. I could clearly see their house in my mind's eye and knew it sat across from where two cottages had once stood. Out of curiosity, Ben researched the history of the land and had discovered that their new home stood on the site where a one-and-a-half cottage had been.

Mandy told me that prior to moving into the house, Katie had always slept through the night. Now, and with increased frequency, Katie would wake up crying and complained of a "bad dream" and that a man was chasing her. While Mandy really wasn't sure what was happening, she knew something wasn't quite right and was definitely listening to her intuition.

After Mandy and Ben spoke to me, I began to feel there was definitely more to Katie's dreams than they at first realized, so I agreed to visit.

It was a cold, damp January evening when I set out for Mandy's home with my team—Karen, a talented medium, Martin, a gifted spiritual and Reiki healer, and Paul.

When we arrived we were greeted by both Mandy and Ben. Katie had been bundled off to her grandmother's home for a visit—something that was quite a treat for her, according to her parents. We walked through the hallway into the lounge, or living room, which was a warm and very inviting space. We stood in these pleasant surrounds and chatted for a while, and Martin made reference to the purpose of our visit. He said he could not feel anything in the room at all; we all nodded in agreement as the energy there was quite pleasant. With her usual stealth Karen chimed in, "There's nothing here; we need to look elsewhere."

We all trooped into the only other downstairs room, a luxurious and spacious kitchen with black marble worktops and a large dining area. Patio doors looked out onto a secluded and landscaped garden.

It was when I walked down the length of the kitchen towards the dining area that I felt as if I had walked through an invisible wall. The density of that space was almost physical.

I silently beckoned the others over for clarification. As they paced out the area, they were able to pinpoint the precise spot where the temperature and energy changed; it ran a path through the dining room table out to the garden from the patio doors.

"What's above here?" I asked, glancing at the others as I spoke.

Mandy replied, "Katie's room."

"That figures," Martin said with a knowing smile.

"Have you ever noticed anything about this room?" I asked Mandy, indicating the room we were standing in.

She smiled and said, "Yeah. It's always bloody cold! We can never warm it up!" She then pointed to the radiator. "Look at the size of that. We had a bigger one put in, but it still has made no difference. No matter what we do, we cannot make it any warmer." As she spoke, Mandy crossed her arms and looked contrite, emphasizing her annoyance at the problem.

"Ben," I asked, "where did you say the other properties stood?" I really didn't need to know the answer because I already knew, but I waited for his response.

"Where you're standing," Ben said, pointing to the areas of cold spots.

I smiled and stopped him. "Don't tell me any more just yet."

The dining room was across from where the old cottage once stood and this gave us the information we needed to continue with our work. I paused and tuned in for a moment when I was suddenly hit with a solid wall of anger that went straight through me. "I'm sorry to be so personal, but I have to ask, have you two been arguing a lot since you moved in here?"

As soon as I asked the question I could see the energy exchange taking place between Mandy and Ben. They looked carefully at one another with smiles on their faces, and then both turned around and in unison said, "Yes."

I was not surprised. I could feel the anger in the ether of the room. I didn't feel this was a result of any angry exchanges between Mandy and Ben, although any arguments they may have had were adding to the cauldron of contempt that was building. And, in fact, as I stood there with my eyes closed I could feel the rage welling up inside me and I wanted to strike out, shout, and throw accusations. When I shared these feelings with the others they agreed. Even Karen, who rarely gets upset, asked to be excused because she felt she might "hit someone."

We all beat a hasty retreat from the room and continued our exploratory investigation upstairs. We purposefully avoided Katie's room as we wanted to leave that for last. We knew we had a serious problem here, but we wanted to find out just how far it extended, so we concentrated our attention on the other two bedrooms and the bathroom. There were no problems in any of these rooms, which were all quiet, calm, and had a gentle energy.

We went back to Katie's bedroom. Even though the room was very pretty and decorated in soft shades of pink, as well as filled with toys and princess furniture that would have delighted any little girl—the heavy atmosphere in the room belied the sweetness of the surroundings.

Our group was standing in the doorway of the room with Mandy and Ben. Suddenly, we sensed a dark and angry energy and honed in on it to find the cause.

There was a man—an extremely angry spirit man in his late fifties who looked to be about 5'6" tall. As soon as we sensed him, we sealed the room with sheafs of light to stop him from escaping. The man was dressed in the style of the 1800s and wearing a dark-brown coat, which was undone. On his feet were boots with the laces loosened. There was coal dust ingrained in his hands that gave away the type of work he had done. He moved about with his arms out by his side and stared and glared at everyone in the room. I began to describe him until Karen finished the description, and then Martin explained the man's personality, and Paul continued with the impact made every time the man entered a room.

Even though this man was enraged, he did begin to talk—or should I say shout—at us. From what we could gather the man had lived in the small cottage that had once stood where Mandy and Ben's house now was. Despite the fact that the physical presence of his original cottage had long since disappeared, the ethereal imprint of the place had not. This man, though dead for a long time, had not realized he was a spirit and continued to remain in his old cottage, albeit in an ethereal sense. As far as he was concerned, Ben and Mandy had built their home over his, and he was furious with them for doing so!

While in the presence of this man, other things began to reveal themselves. He had been a father to many children when he and his family had lived in this very small cottage. He had been a hard worker, a drinker, and a wife beater who had lived his life through cruel actions and harsh emotions. After years of being in a void he had now found someone to unleash his pent-up emotions on, and that person was Katie. Fortunately, at three years of age she couldn't figure out the difference between a dream state and being awake—so she was interpreting the man's presence and atrocious behavior as a bad dream.

As we continued to communicate with the man, he was constantly trying to shoo us out of the bedroom, and he used every trick in the book to make us leave what he felt was his personal space. This, then, was what he had been doing to Katie—shooing her out of her own bedroom— and now it was understood why Katie had been going into her parents' room several nights a week, crying and refusing to go back to her bed. And this was also why the child had been saying things like "nasty man" and "bad man"—complaints her parents had put down to nightmares.

As we worked with this man—who truly did not realize he was dead—we learned that as far as he was concerned, Ben, Mandy, and Katie were in his house and he wanted them out, and out now!

The man began speaking through Karen and when she repeated what he was saying his rage increased. "Get them out! Get these bloody people out of my house now!" he shouted. He then turned on us. "What are you doing here? Who bloody invited you?"

We tried to reason with him, but he was having none of it, and we decided we had had enough.

We already had him sealed in the room and we had Mandy and Ben's permission to command his departure. We were almost positive he wouldn't leave of his own accord, so we began to mentally create a doorway through which the other side could enter.

As soon as we began the process, Martin reported seeing the man's mother standing in the doorway with a glow around her and her arms outstretched as she welcomed her son home.

I urged the man to look at his mother. She appeared as a short, stout woman wearing a gray dress that went to the floor, and the dress was covered with a crisp, white apron. She continued to hold her arms out to the man and beckon him to her. Then the man looked at his mother and all of us could feel his energy soften as he soaked in the vision of her standing there waiting for him. Before our eyes the tough, angry man began to melt because her love for him diminished his negative emotions.

This was exactly the break we needed and nothing else was required. Spirit helpers came and gently pushed him towards his mother and, after only a few moments, it was all over. He was back where he belonged.

Just minutes after the man was sent over, Katie's bedroom and the dining area began to feel decidedly warmer. Each of us felt this positive physical change. However, as a precaution, we created spheres—mini tornadoes of vibrant energy—and sent them around the room to remove any residual negative energy.

This spirit had not realized he was dead; he had simply lived on in his ethereal cottage, and then Ben, Mandy, and Katie moved in. For eighteen months their two worlds had collided and he had spent the majority of that time trying to drive them out. So rather than this lost soul moving into their home and haunting them, they had, in effect, moved into his. And they had failed to ask his permission to do so.

The Alcoholic Ghost

My friend Sharon asked if we would visit a former work colleague named Becky, who had only been living in her apartment for about five months. At age twenty-seven, this was Becky's first place of her own and, even though she was sharing it with her boyfriend Pete, the apartment was in her name and represented her independence. However, the disturbances occurring on a regular basis had quickly turned the dream place into a living nightmare. Because of this, Becky had called in an amateur ghost hunter.

As soon as I had a chance to speak to Becky I knew without a doubt that she had paranormal activity in her home. It first started with her having uncomfortable feelings, then came odd sounds, scratching, banging, and the sound of an occasional sigh. The visit by the amateur ghost hunter had only escalated everything. Shortly after the ghost hunter visit the activity increased to include other noises, such as creaking of the set of leather furniture, even though it was unoccupied. Becky said she was also constantly awakened during the night by her bedroom door opening and the sensation that someone was standing very close to her. Sometimes she reported she felt a gentle breeze across her face, which gave her the impression someone was breathing just inches away from her. Further, arguments between her and Pete were occurring on a regular basis and she thought the tension was causing both of them to drink more than was good for them.

Our team was greeted at the door by Pete and we were led directly to the living room, where we found Becky sitting with her mother on the sofa.

A few moments after we began to work, Becky's best friend Michelle arrived and plunked herself down on the settee directly in front of us. This intrusion really bothered me, and I felt extremely annoyed with Michelle and wanted to tell her to leave. As this feeling was a little irrational for me, I thought it warranted a bit more tuning into. Sure enough, as soon as I did this I could clearly see a rotund African-Caribbean spirit man wearing a hat and coat with a cardigan zipped up to the top. He was on the settee—and Michelle had sat right down on top of him!

Before I could relay this information, Karen, a medium on our team, began to talk about another male spirit who was in the apartment. I had already sensed the other presence and here was the confirmation. I then explained to Michelle and Becky about the entity that liked to sit where Michelle was presently seated. She very quickly jumped up and changed places, seating herself as far away from me as she could.

It should be noted that there was a distinct difference in energy and temperature in the living room. We could feel that there were two places of extreme cold here and we would come back and address this in a while, but right now we knew we had to address the problem in Becky's bedroom, where she had been subjected to nightly disturbances such as the bedroom door opening and closing and the feeling that someone was breathing close to her.

In Becky's room I immediately sensed a small, dark-haired man in his sixties and Karen quickly confirmed this. Our team member Martin joined in and spoke of the spirit man's drinking problem. Karen felt it was likely the man had drunk himself to death. We all sensed there was no connection between the occupants of this apartment or the spirit man. This was a wandering and lost soul who was not at all interested in Becky or Pete—everything that drove this man was alcohol-based. Even though he had passed on, he was still addicted to the source, and now he was trapped here. Unlike other entities, he was not attracted to or repelled by anyone—his only draw was to alcohol.

It was ascertained that this lost soul had wandered in and may have wandered out on his own if not for the visit of the ghost hunter, who had given the spirit a significant amount of power. Now that he was in residence, he had been using his newly gained power to unduly influence the new occupants.

I decided to test this theory. I asked, "Becky, did you tell me you have been drinking more since you moved here?"

"Not so much on weekdays," she replied, "but on weekends." Then she added, "And now that you mention it, during the week as well, and more recently." She had more to tell us. "Do you know, the other night I was in bed reading and Pete brought me a vodka and coke at 11:30 at night?" She told us that she hadn't asked for a drink and didn't fancy one, so she asked Pete what he thought he was playing at, and why he had brought the drink when she was about to go to sleep. Pete told her he had clearly heard her calling him and asking him to pour her the drink.

At first Becky stated she had tried to argue with Pete, but he was adamant about her calling out for a vodka and coke.

"Did you drink it?" I asked.

"Yeah," Becky replied. "I wasn't going to waste it," she said with a smile.

Her face then changed expression as she suddenly realized what had happened. "Was that *him*?" she asked, referring to the alcoholic ghost. "I would never drink in bed normally."

We had to admit the spirit man was the probable influence. We quickly secured Becky's permission and could now begin the process of removing the entity from the apartment.

Of course, the spirit man did not want to go. He was very frightened of where he might end up and this was most likely due to the fact that, after his passing, he had wandered around for quite a while before settling here and he found it to his liking. Yet, as the warmth from the doorway we had opened began to percolate through, he relaxed a little and then he effortlessly moved towards the warmth and the glowing light. All of his fears appeared to fade as he moved into the light. I felt certain that once he was on the other side he would be given the help he needed to rid himself of the driving urge for alcohol. He would, I knew, be weaned away from drink and his soul restored.

As always, we could feel the difference in the room as the soul moved to the other side.

We now returned to the living room to deal with the other ghostly occupant. We tuned in and almost immediately found the Jamaican-born gentleman seated on the settee. He was in the same spot we had seen him earlier, but this time he appeared very relaxed and unaffected by our presence. It was felt his relaxed manner gave some indication that he at one time had a connection to this apartment. He was very easy to talk to, and he politely answered all our questions.

Very gently we began to explain to him that his presence was frightening Becky. He was a real gentleman and seemed quite put out that he had caused Becky any distress. He apologized and explained in a broad Jamaican accent, "This is me lounge." Then, without any further prompting from us, he stood up and tipped his hat in a gesture of farewell. He then walked over to the doorway we had created, mumbled a few more apologies, and in a moment he was gone.

Once the man was gone, we then quickly turned our attention to the large cold spot in the middle of the living room. Here we found a crossover point, or "node" between two ley lines. Ley lines are energy lines that traverse the planet. They are pathways where the veil between the two worlds is at its thinnest. This is an extremely powerful earth energy doorway and, provided that it is clean of negative energies, it can be a wonderful zone to have in a home. If it is not clean, it can create a living hell as it is a point where interaction between the two worlds is more likely to occur.

In this case, we visualized the area covered with powerful white light and manipulated the energy until the node was clear. As we did this we could see a bright beam of light begin to shine out of the ground. We then double-checked around the apartment. In a short amount of time the air in the place was much clearer and the rooms seemed brighter.

We bid our goodbyes and hurried out into the cold air. Karen was the first out and, as she stood waiting for the rest of the group, she commented on how much happier the ground felt following the clearing and capping of the node. I stood in the freezing cold and tuned into the property and had to agree with Karen that the ground underneath our feet did feel happier, because it was flowing with vibrant energy.

I must remark that I am sure the amateur ghost hunter who came to the apartment did not set out to cause Becky and Pete any harm or distress. But, we are unfortunately living in dangerous times as ghost hunting becomes the norm.

What is termed "fright entertainment" as seen on television in recent years fails to show the dangers of interacting with something one cannot fully understand.

Two

Two

Haunted Tales

We continue with more tales of ghosts and demons. Here you will find a creepy clown doll, a cupboard that conceals something bad, the present-day effects of an ancient witch coven, and even the dire effects of a popular television show.

An Evil Man Afraid of Nothing

Annette called asking for assistance with an unwanted ghost that was haunting her and her family. She explained that she had gotten my number from a couple her husband had bumped into—a couple I had, coincidentally, done a house clearing for the day prior.

Annette's tone was fast-paced and pleading, "Can you come soon? My children are terrified. My daughters won't sleep in their own room. My little boy is afraid to go to bed and now I have all three of them trying to sleep in the box room (a smaller bedroom). My husband and I are arguing all the time and the children fight constantly. They are being tormented by a toy clown that keeps them awake by laughing during the night!"

She went on to explain that there had been a physical attack on her eldest daughter. And Annette said she could feel the presence of a man, mainly in the upstairs.

I promised to do whatever I could to help.

We arrived at the property a few days later on a cold, rainy evening for a pre-visit, which was brief. The home was around eighty years old, and Annette and husband Michael had lived in the house for about three years—but their troubles hadn't developed until the last four months.

With the children away and visiting elsewhere we walked around the house; our instincts told us to start upstairs. We found that the parents' room was at the front of the house, as was the little boy's room. The girls shared a double room at the rear of the house.

The box room was the only room that felt okay to us. The parents' room was a little uncomfortable, but it was nothing at all like the girls' room, and so we decided to start in the room we felt was the hub of activity.

The girls' room was full of girlie things. Bunk beds were set up in the corner and pink princess was the theme throughout the place. In the corner was a built-in cupboard, and a chest of drawers sat against the door of the cupboard blocking access to it. Scattered around the room was an array of cuddly toys. In other words, on the surface this was a typical children's bedroom.

As soon as we walked into the room, Karen looked at a large clown doll sitting on a pile of other toys. She said, "I don't like that."

We all turned to look at this "innocent-looking" doll and found we agreed. It looked like Chucky, the demonic doll from the movies. The grin on its face could only be described as sinister. We decided to deal with the doll later.

"For some reason I don't like this cupboard," Paul said. "I can't explain why, but I don't."

Annette added, "Neither do the children. They are convinced something horrible lives in there. That's why the chest of drawers is in front of it."

We watched as Martin opened the cupboard door. When we looked inside the cupboard it appeared to be very dark. The color of the cupboard was the same as the room—pastel pink, yet, in my mind's eye it appeared to be unpainted plaster that was dark, cracked, and covered in dirt and cobwebs. I sensed I was seeing this cupboard as it had appeared many years ago, and I was very glad when Martin shut the door.

We were still not sure what we were dealing with, but we could all feel a presence—we were just unsure at this stage if this was to be a rescue or banishment. In order to determine this, we stood together in a circle and I invited whatever was residing in the upper floor of the house to come talk to us.

I felt a male presence draw close. He was quite short in stature and in his late forties. He was overweight with greasy hair—and worse than that, I could smell the alcohol and stale tobacco coming off him. He swaggered in with his belt in his hand as if he were looking for trouble. Most entities will quickly realize the potential of mediums to send them on their way and will hide from them. Not this one! He was too arrogant to think we could do anything to him. We sensed this spirit man had no connections to anyone in the house—he had simply wandered in and found fresh victims.

He honed in on Karen almost immediately, seeming to believe she was the weakest link. But tonight Karen was not buying it! Something about this man's persona brought out the best in her and she came out fighting. "He's trying to overpower me," she said with a degree of hesitancy in her voice. Then more firmly, "Well, bring it on!" She changed her stance as she pulled in her own power. "This man is using foul language and he wants to know what you lot are doing here." None of us rose to the bait.

Then he bounced off onto me. He hit my chest and I felt myself jump back from the intensity of the energy he was pummeling me with.

"He's over here with me!" I said. I then exerted my power back to show him I could not be overcome. I challenged him to try, but he did not. The entity did not attempt to bother the men, but instead returned his attention to Karen, who was still unfazed by the energy he was sending her way.

Karen began to explain some of what she felt about the man. "This man was so angry when he was alive and feels he has been robbed of life in his prime. He is not ready to go anywhere."

It seemed a total waste of time to try to lure him to crossover with a loved one, because as far as he was concerned, he wasn't going anywhere, even though I did explain to him that he was not welcome here and was frightening the children. He merely sneered at my words.

The team and I looked at one another and nodded. We created a silver doorway by one of the windows. We then opened the doorway and gently pushed him through. He was not at all for going, and it took several minutes before every inch of his ethereal body was well and truly through. As soon as he disappeared we could, as usual, feel the physical change in the room. The atmosphere was better and the space felt much lighter than before.

Now we had to take care of sinister-looking clown doll. We neutralized it and removed the evil energy that encompassed it. Then, as a precaution, we put out waves of energy across the whole of the top floor from one room to another to remove any residual energy and replaced what was there with a much more vibrant ambience.

As we finished up Annette asked, "Could I have caused someone to have a miscarriage?"

"I'm not sure what you are asking me. Can you explain?" I responded.

Annette then told me the story. She said she often had premonitions and occasionally things would just come to her. A few months ago she told a friend that she thought the friend was pregnant. It turned out Annette was correct as the friend was nearly three months along. Four weeks later the friend miscarried.

As Annette lay on her bed one night, a being came to her and told her that her friend had lost the baby because of her. As Annette relayed this story to us she realized this could not be true and that whatever entity had spoken to her had only created self-doubt. She was not to blame for the miscarriage.

I never heard from Annette again, although I did learn through the church that the children had returned to their home and had shouted, "No more nasty man! No more nasty man!"

Out of the mouths of babes.

A Witch's Coven

Jackie found me by chance.

In desperation she had visited a Mind, Body, and Spirit shop in Dudley, England, in search of amulets she could use to frighten away the unseen forces that had been terrorizing her family. The shop owner put her in touch with me.

Jackie lived with her husband James and their twelve-year-old son Jake. They had been living in their present home for over nine years, but within the last year the situation had gotten out of hand. The boy complained of being pushed and pulled day and night, and this was in addition to being awakened at night by a terrifying presence that seemed to hover over him as he lay in his bed. Now their son refused to go to bed in his room and was sleeping on the sofa downstairs.

Jackie reported seeing faces in the floor and having a terrible sense of being watched whenever she was in the bathroom.

Jackie was also convinced that something or someone was whispering to her and warning her of her husband's plans to cheat on her. While James was a non-believer in otherworldly things, he did note that on several occasions he had stepped out of the shower and found himself covered in scratches that ran from his shoulders all down the front and back of his body—and for these scratches he had no explanation. Despite these encounters, James refused to acknowledge that anything was wrong and did his best to rationalize the whole situation, mostly by ignoring it and remaining in denial.

Aware of James's stance on the matter, my team and I attended the property. My team on this trip consisted of Beverley, a psychic and energy worker; Patrick, a talented light worker, Reiki Master, and psychic; and Lyn, a gifted medium, Angelic Reiki Master, and extremely powerful energy worker.

When we got there, it was noted that James's color was awful and something was clearly draining him of his life energy. We determined we would definitely deal with this as soon as we could. Despite James's disbelief, I felt he was a key player and therefore we needed him on the site. It is very important that everyone we work with have an open mind. The darkness will feed on the mind of the non-believer as a means to thwart our efforts. James was more than extremely frank about his views, but said he would try to have an open mind throughout our visit. He did keep his word to us.

As the majority of the activity appeared to happen on the upper floor, it seemed to be the logical place for us to start. Within a short while, we realized the heart of the action was indeed in the bathroom. In fact, no sooner did we enter this room than James reported feeling as if the floor were giving away and he seemed to be having difficulty maintaining his balance. We could all feel a change in energy close to the tub, as if we had entered into another dimension. This feeling ran through the entire back of the house, through their son's bedroom, and also through the kitchen and dining room.

We decided to concentrate on clearing the upper floor of negative entities or vibrations and would deal with the lower floors as soon as we could.

We moved into the front bedroom and were immediately surrounded by extreme cold. This room, despite its lovely floral decoration and soft pastel colors, seemed home to a dark and foreboding energy that felt as though it were embedded in the atmosphere.

We placed everyone in strategic points around the room and began to tune in.

There was a strong feminine energy here.

Dark shadows constantly floated about the room in snakelike movements.

Lyn stood with her energy open and inviting, welcoming this darkness to communicate through her. While Lyn held the vibration, we worked as one. I also linked in to this fiendish feminine entity and quickly felt the cunning of it as it played and toyed with us. It began speaking of its evil deeds and how it weaved itself into James's dreams and had become a beautiful deity that toyed with him, presenting her beauty to steal his love from Jackie. The entity bragged about how she had gone to Jackie and told her of her husband's deceit.

James was absolutely amazed by what we were revealing.

Now we had gathered all the information we needed from the entity and we began to push her back to her own world. Lyn held onto the energy as the group worked together. With a huge surge of energy, we pushed the entity through a darkened doorway, back to where she belonged, and then we closed the vortex in the bathroom by engulfing it in golden light. We then collectively neutralized the power of a tornado of energy by slowing it down and reducing it in depth and height until it slowly stopped rotating. Once it ceased, we used the golden light as a blanket to seal the opening where it had originated and swept the upper floor with renewed vibration.

It was now time to move downstairs and clear whatever else had penetrated into our world.

We were drawn into the small kitchen to a spot directly below the bathroom. It would seem a lot of activity had occurred since this extension to the home had been added.

Almost immediately Beverley sensed rituals had been done a long time ago on the land. Lyn also shared her vision of circles of women performing some sort of Wicca that belonged to the dark side. Every one of us sensed the pentagram embedded in the land. From this we deduced this house sat close to or on the site of a former witch's coven and the extension on the house had somehow closed the gap between the two times.

The evil force was quickly drawn to Lyn and the power from this force was immense. It was too much for us to handle. We then began to work in unison with the other side and became a conductor for them.

Slowly the energy poured in and built up around Lyn, and the room became darker as she became the focal point for this force. I urged the others to look away as we loaned our energy to the other side. We could feel the power surging through Lyn, tempting us to acknowledge it and become part of it. Again I urged the others not to look at Lyn or accept the entity's existence.

Thankfully, we only needed to resist the force for a few minutes, because in a short span of time it was gone, hopefully banished forever.

As I felt the negative energy subside I became aware that the family dog had come into the kitchen. The dog stood mesmerized, motionless. The dog was in such shock that it urinated, then sat in its own urine. After the energy was cleared, the dog returned to normal.

We moved out into the garden and found that here, buried in the land, was the imprint of long-lost rituals and a place where portals had been opened into another world. These imprints still remained active, unfettered and forgotten magic in motion that continued to do horrible work. With a golden light, we closed off this portal by reversing the magic performed all those years ago, and the bridge was sealed forever.

Finally we turned our attention to James, who appeared ashen in color, as if the life blood had, over many months, been drained out of him. He complained of chronic tiredness, headaches, and general aches and pains. Collectively, we psychically scanned his energy field, moving left to right across his body like a scanning machine, searching for some anomaly that would tell us there was a blockage, a dark concentration of energy. Or an attachment embedded into his etheric body, designed to drain his life energy to feed so dark a force. If these attachments are left in place they can cause the victim serious harm as their physical body is drained of its life force. Once we found these on James, we deftly removed them by replacing them with healing vibrations; we also replenished his energy.

It took a couple of weeks for James to begin to feel the benefits of that night. It was only after he began to recover that he realized how very ill he had been.

Most Haunted Live–Almost

By the time I returned Lesley's call, she had phoned me three times in the space of twelve hours, speaking to both my partner and my answering machine. She was desperate for the group to come out as soon as possible. She told me that her daughter Angie was at a breaking point and her grandchildren were terrified.

The list of occurrences seemed endless. A large, battery-operated clock had begun ticking loudly in the granddaughter's bedroom, but it had no batteries in it. Baskets of shoes were upturned in seconds. Angie had been lying in bed reading one night when she saw a man's form in a beaded curtain. This was in addition to the loud banging that came from above her head and jolted her out of sleep.

Lesley noted that Angie's youngest boy slept alone. At age two he did not quite have a command of the English language, but when asked what was in his room he screwed up his face, bared his teeth, and made clawlike shapes with his hands. He would also make snarling sounds and move about as if showing that someone were rushing at him.

The other two grandsons who shared a bedroom kept waking up in the night, shouting and screaming, "Bad man! Bad man!"

Until recently all the activity had been centered around Angie and the other children. The only encounter that Angie's husband John had experienced involved an ashtray floating away from him while he was using it.

There was no mistake—something was growing strong, and very quickly, from the fear it was harvesting from Angie and the children—and now it apparently felt able to tackle the man of the house.

I assembled a team of Karen, Martin, and Paul. We were accompanied to the site by Gary, an amateur ghost hunter, who brought along his wife Tracey.

The house was a semi-detached council house (public housing) that had been built in the 1930s. Externally there was nothing untoward to be noted and certainly no telltale signs of what the family had been exposed to over the last six or so weeks.

We were greeted at the door by Lesley, Angie, and John. For this evening, Angie's children were in the care of their grandfather, who lived just across the road.

Angie was clearly in an extreme nervous state. Her face was pale and drawn and she held her cardigan close to her body, as if keeping something from penetrating. I could see what an ordeal this was for her because her apprehension was so high—indeed for the majority of the time we were there she was physically shaking and occasionally burst out in tears. All of us knew that in her present state it would not take very much for her to ask us to stop our work.

The group concluded that the entity had targeted Angie as the weakest link and was now trying everything it could to impress her to make us go away—but of course that was not going to happen.

Before we began, we stood and laughed and joked for a few moments, doing our best to get Angie to relax and, by the end of that time, she appeared to be a tiny bit more at peace than she had been when we first arrived. We reassured her that by the time we left, the property would be back to how it was before all the disturbances started; this news seemed to calm her a bit more. What we didn't want was for her to feel she couldn't go through with this, because if that happened the victory would be for the entity. Meanwhile, Angie's husband John seemed at a loss over what to do. He appeared to be both distraught and angry at the prospect that there was nothing he could do to shield his family from this evil onslaught.

We now began our walk around the downstairs. We felt the living room was not a problem, but the same could not be said for the kitchen. Angie confirmed our views on this area, stating that every time she came into the kitchen she felt she was being watched.

Gary now moved in with his thermometer and ERF meter—a measurement device that gives a strong reading whenever psychic activity is nearby. As Gary ran the ERF meter around the kitchen, it began to shoot off the scale, mainly by the gas cooker. The temperature was a steady 22 degrees Celsius except where the cooker stood—here the temperature dropped to 14 degrees Celsius. There was no logical explanation for this. In fact, near the cooker we all experienced a slight tingling sensation. Angie eagerly confirmed this was the exact spot where she often felt an intimidating and frightening something was watching her. As soon as she said this, a sudden blast of icy cold air shot past us. Before I had a chance to speak, Angie asked, "Did anyone feel that?" Every one of us confirmed that we had.

As a group we realized what had just happened—the cold blast of air was the entity rushing out of the kitchen before we could pin it down.

We immediately went through the house, starting at the girl's bedroom. In view of the activity around it, the room seemed the ideal starting point and was where the entity had rushed off to. Angie seated herself on the bed between her mom and Tracey. Gary positioned himself close to the door so he could take pictures until we began the actual clearance.

The entity felt very male and dominant, and we began to try to communicate with it. Most times a spirit such as this has simply lost its way and just needs guidance and reassurance that it's safe to go through the doorway. Not this one. He was determined to stay put. The entity quickly proved to be very angry. As far as he was concerned, he was going nowhere.

All of us in the group sensed this being was alien to our world because of the emotions and vibrations we were picking up from him. Still, we began to talk to him. Karen and I created a picture of him as we spoke. He appeared covered in wild hair with a hideous-looking face. Everything about him was almost troll-like, except that, at over five feet, he was much taller than the usual concept of a troll.

Suddenly Karen's face began to contort, her persona became menacing, and profanity came from her mouth. "I'm going nowhere!" she spat out. "You don't know what you're messing with!" Her voice was ominous. She turned to glare at me and I could feel the venom dripping from her words as she spoke. Her gaze locked onto mine. The waves of hatred pouring from her were powerful as the beast worked through her to try its best to overpower me.

As Karen spoke, she kept stepping towards me in a lunging motion as if she were going to physically attack me. Each lunge threw waves of fear through me. I quelled the fear each time as this elongated troll and I fell into psychic combat. Every one of its lunges forward hit me in my solar plexus and I batted it back.

The solar plexus chakra is a very important one. It is the seat of our personal power. From here, energy is channeled to the rest of the body. In Sanskrit this energy center is called Manipura and is said to be the center of etheric-psychic intuition. Entities and demons will attack this area in an attempt to disarm us, or as a means to harm us, by draining the body of physical power. It can also be a means of or a point for attacking us psychically.

Despite Karen's actions to do harm, she did maintain control over the entity—but just barely. We decided that enough was enough.

We opened the doorway and tried to entice the entity through, but it remained clear that no persuading on our part was going to get him to go through voluntarily. Then White Feather came and instructed the group to create a tunnel of energy and push the entity down the tunnel and through the doorway to his home.

The being stood facing me with the tunnel directly behind him and, as I stepped forward, he reluctantly stepped backward, getting closer to the tunnel; the power from the spirit was strong enough to influence me. As I walked past Martin I suddenly felt very angry with him and had an incredible urge to turn and punch him. This was just another ploy by this beast to break my concentration so that he could get free. I ignored the feelings and continued to push him towards the opening.

A few moments later he was gone into the tunnel and we all breathed a sigh of relief.

As always we spent some time filling the bedrooms with positive energy using Mexican waves. By the time we were finished we had filled every room in the house with positive vibrations. When this was done we all returned to the living room and it was there that I raised the question about the use of the Ouija board.

The family was adamant that they did not approve of such things. Lesley did tell us the closest anyone had come to a Ouija board was when they had seen one used on a popular television program, *Most Haunted Live*. From the timeline stated it would appear that their problems had begun precisely at that point. It was Angie and John who had been alone in the house and viewed the spooky entertainment show. John had said he thought it was a load of rubbish, and no sooner had he finished his sentence when the living room door suddenly slammed shut with tremendous force. By report the force was so intense that the whole house had reverberated with the sound. The next day the banging disturbances and terrorizing of the children began.

I admit I am no expert on this subject, but it certainly made all of us think. Had watching the TV show somehow invited this entity in? Had the television program somehow acted as a conduit—a doorway—for the entity to traverse between the two worlds?

I now began to suspect the watching of a live program about the paranormal might be seen as an invitation to various entities. I don't know how this happened, but what I do know is this—after that fateful day a perfectly normal household became a hotbed of mega-paranormal activity.

Powered by Others

As I have stated many times before, the rescue or banishment of unwanted and unseen entities is a very serious undertaking. Once we begin the process it has to be completed, otherwise the power created goes to the dark side. There are several things that can lead to failure—one is being unable to detect the entity, either because it is hiding so well or the medium simply does not have the skill to find it. A further block can be that the disembodied spirit is too powerful for the psychic workers. In any case the probability is that the aborted attempt will fuel the problems the family or person involved are facing. The inability to complete the clearing or banishment of the entity turns the power over to the dark forces and they will use it to wreak havoc on their victims. This was the case with our next call.

What had begun with little taps and bangs that could have been viewed as annoyances had evolved into physical attacks that included hair pulled to the point of physical hurt and large chunks of hair falling out in a mysterious way. The family involved spoke of being unable to breathe when they went upstairs and there was further talk of a dark, ominous figure that terrified anyone who visited the property. Other things were also disturbing—ethereal cats and dogs crying and baying long into the night. There was the sound of babies crying pitifully and children calling out for help. Footsteps would also be heard walking up and down the landing, and occasionally doors would slam viciously shut. In the back bedroom the wallpaper had been pulled off two of the walls and small pieces lay in piles as if they had floated down. At one point it had been thought that dampness in the house had caused the wallpaper to come loose, but tests and inspections done at the site had proven this was not the case.

The daily onslaught generated such fear in this household by the that the sixteen-year-old son had moved out and refused to return until the problem was resolved.

We got as many of our group together as possible, which included mediums Bill, Lyn and I, Paul, and Patrick—a talented light worker, Reiki Master, and psychic. We agreed to meet at the site.

For once I was the first to arrive on that fine Saturday night. While I waited for the others, I mentally placed the house in a holding vibration. I scanned the row of houses and in my mind's eye saw rolling purple clouds that faded in and out. I watched as these ethereal clouds rose high above the house and flowed down the street. I knew then that we had a ley line—and because of the purple color I knew it was a negative one at that—and these houses sat right across from it.

The mother lived in a mid-terraced home with the eldest son, who was nineteen—the sixteen-year-old was still out of the house. The family had lived on the property only a couple of weeks when the problems began. There was, by report, not one part of the site where activity had not been seen, sensed, or felt. On the night of our visit the mother and eldest son were present.

After walking around and scanning the house's interior we decided to start off in the back bedroom. Two further piles of wallpaper had appeared since yesterday and the piles were located near the wall. Within moments Patrick and Paul began to cough. We placed the mother and her son in a protective zone in the room and began to tune in. It wasn't long before a very agitated and frightened male spirit came to join us, and this seemed to cause the coughing to increase, with Lyn now joining in.

Bill started the dialogue, "Sandrea, I have a man standing to my left." Then Bill fell silent, instinctively knowing that he needed to say no more. Lyn stood quietly reading the vibes.

"How old do you think the man is?" I asked.

Lyn didn't look at me as she continued to focus her concentration. She answered, "Mid- to late fifties."

I turned to Bill, who nodded in agreement, as did Patrick. This, of course, was precisely what I was seeing myself. A man, slightly built at about 5'6", dark hair, and in his mid-fifties. Now that we all had him in our sights, we could move forward.

Lyn slowly began to change her stance. She moved her feet slightly to adjust her weight distribution and then she placed her hands behind her back with her hands grasping each wrist. She needed no encouragement or prompting. Lyn recognized that this man wished to communicate with someone, and she had decided it was going to be her. There was no need for words between us. Lyn looked over at me and I nodded and smiled in approval, and then Lyn got on with the task at hand.

"This man is very, very angry," she said before again adjusting her position as the entity stepped closer to her—but she was keeping him at arm's length.

Lyn said, "He keeps repeating 'it was not my fault. It was not my fault. I didn't mean to do it.'"

Bill caught my attention from across the room. He mouthed to me, "It was a fire."

I nodded in agreement.

Lyn went on to report that the man had died in a fire that started in a chip pan (a deep-sided cooking pan used for making French fries). Apparently he had come home late at night, put the chip pan on the gas stove, and promptly fell asleep. Unfortunately, this man was not the only one who lost his life that day. Forty years later, he was still trapped here, held by fear.

Lyn allowed the man to move closer, and slowly their energies merged so they were as one. The spirit was now using Lyn to communicate with us.

"I'm sorry, I didn't mean it," he repeated several times. "Will you tell them I'm sorry?" he pleaded.

Lyn's eyes looked moist as he explained his pity over his actions. Together we communicated with him that the fire may have been caused by him, but it didn't matter now—it was how he had chosen to leave this dimension.

At this we all realized this was truly the rescue of a lost soul. As he continued to talk, we all became aware of his mother; she appeared as a shimmering blue form and she stood in a silver doorway. Her eyes locked onto Lyn's and she radiated the most wonderful smile to her lost son.

Hesitantly at first, he started to disengage from Lyn and slowly edged closer to the doorway.

For all intents and purposes our work should have been complete when the man went through the doorway, but it was not. It was clear to us there were several other entities in the house. The energy still felt dark and foreboding on this floor, and this was always a strong indication that matters had not been totally resolved.

Multiple hauntings are quite rare, and when they occur, they are usually associated with either demons or beings brought through by the use of a Ouija board. For the latter reason, I turned to the son and asked, "I hope you don't mind me asking, but we need to know—have you or your brother used a Ouija board here in this house?"

"Yes," he replied, as if I had simply asked the time of day. "A few months ago my brother and a few of our friends did try to find out who was in the house."

Knowing glances shot among all of us in the group.

"That's okay," I said, but I would talk to him afterwards about the Ouija board. In the meantime, we needed to deal with the problems in the house.

Downstairs we found it—a very powerful force. It was a huge, dark entity that had positioned itself behind the television. This entity felt like what can only be described as a foreboding shadow. Motionless, it cast a shadow that permeated through the whole house. As if to make a point, the mother's bedroom door gave a mighty bang as it slammed shut.

"Did you hear that?" asked the mother.

Of course, we couldn't help but hear it as the whole house shook.

Somehow this entity seemed to have the ability to spread and reach out into each of the rooms in the house while all the time it remained rooted to the spot behind the television.

The family had been blighted by seeing black shadows everywhere, including in their sleep, and this entity was the creator. In the shadows he could create illusions—the crying babies and children, the screaming cats and baying dogs—none of these existed in real time, but were only shadows and sounds that were created to disturb all those who saw or heard them. This also extended to the hair pulling that had been occurring—in fact, nearly all the activity in the house was being generated by this sinister shadow.

We knew mere mortals were no match for such a fiend, and so we made no attempt to communicate with the entity. We had discovered it but made no move to acknowledge its existence—we would leave this to the other side, knowing the spirit workers would do their job and that we were merely their earthly contact points.

We received the mother's permission to remove the entity and, as she fully approved, we began the process as usual. After a few frightening and hair-raising moments the being was finally dissolved and returned to the place it came from. It was remarkable to watch the guides at work and I could see the huge shadow begin to fade, as if pulled through some unseen doorway. While this went on, we all held the vibrational space in silence, offering this darkness nothing. Finally it was over, and a cool breeze, an increase in light, and a white feather drifting down gave us the all clear.

Hindsight is a wonderful thing, and after this we realized we should have dealt with the black shadow first, but we hadn't. It soon became apparent the man who had set the chip pan fire had been pulled back from the light. The dark shadow, having held him captive here for the last few months, had still exerted control over him. As the man had begun his journey home, the shadow had enticed him back. The man was not strong enough to fight the calling of this darkness and, despite the draw of his own mother coming for him, he had returned to the house. Now he was panicking. The shadow had gone and now the man was desperate and sure he had missed his call home.

"The man is back again," Lyn said. "I can feel him to my right."

Without warning the spirit jumped into Lyn's aura without asking or receiving her permission—truly a cowardly act. Lyn was not at all prepared for this, but, the professional she is, she said nothing. We watched as she adjusted her stance, placed her arms behind her back, and held her wrists with her hands. Slowly and deliberately she locked her gaze onto mine. The dark light that shone out of what had been Lyn's eyes was not hers. The entity, convinced he had lost all hope of going home, radiated nothing but anger. We could feel his rage radiating out of Lyn's aura.

We flew into action and began the process of removing the spirit and again making preparations for the entity to be returned to his own world. It didn't take long before the other side sprang into action and we could all feel a breeze move through the area as they began their work. It almost felt as if a spirit police force had been sent to arrest the man. The easy way had already been tried—that of enticing him with his mother—but now this entity was becoming a danger to Lyn.

Soon I sensed White Feather use his coat of feathers to sweep through Lyn's energy field and take the entity away. Normally when this happens, there is a sensation of spirits rising up towards the light—but not on this occasion. This entity was pushed backward and then diagonally down towards the floor. It was held there in the grip of two white beings before shooting through a window of light with a spirit worker on either side. At the moment of exit, Lyn almost lost her balance as the energy swept through her and the entity was literally knocked out of her aura. We all instantly sensed the point when

Lyn was clear of this spirit, and we gave her a few moments to recover before moving on.

A quick check of the house was carried out and an energy exchange performed throughout the property. When we walked into the front room we heard a little bird singing. The son went over to a bird cage and removed the cover. The boy looked at the bird fondly and told us that the bird had not sung in weeks.

With the house restored back to normal, we spent a few moments talking to the mother and son about the dangers of using a Ouija board without proper training or experience. Both of them seemed unaware of anything negative being associated with using this type of tool. The son appeared a little confused by what we were saying and explained that they had only done what they had seen mediums do on the TV ghost programs. The mom leapt to her son's defense and told us she had witnessed the board being used correctly by the boys. "It's not a Ouija board," she said. "It's glass divination."

It is often so difficult to explain to people some of the perils inherent in the Ouija board, especially when they are seen on a weekly basis on popular television shows. What is even more difficult is trying to convey the link between the actions of using the board and the trauma that can follow, because whatever has been let in by using the board takes a little while to build sufficient power before it is detected. Therefore, it is not always easy for many to recognize the connection between the use of the board and the onset of paranormal activity, as any entities coming through will take some time learning how to operate in this dimension. Then the entity will move its focus to harvesting energy through fear.

And, yes, I am aware there are many who do use the Ouija board skillfully and as a wonderful tool of communicating with spirits—it is just that my team and I have seen the opposite of the good results when the board is used.

Three

Even More
Haunted Tales

Sometimes those who do a bit of amateur ghost hunting upset the spirits and cause some disturbances in the lives of those whose homes they investigate. Here are instances of a psychic unknowingly depositing a ghost in a home, and even a bit of Voodoo!

Take Your Rubbish Home with You!
Vera, at the prompting of her youngest daughter, decided to host a psychic party at her house.

After the party was over it was noted that while everyone had appeared to have a pleasant time, some were a little disappointed by the standard of mediumship they had experienced.

For Vera, however, it seemed her life would never be the same again.

Long after the medium was gone, a ghostly presence haunted her family. Vera and her husband Derek had lived in the family home for over five years, and there had never been any issues or problems with ghosts before. That was until the visit by the medium who did the readings in the home—and that was when the trouble began.

Vera constantly had the sensation that something was watching her. No matter where she was in the house, she had no peace, as this thing seemed to follow her everywhere. On one occasion, while in the living room, she had caught sight of a ghostly figure standing by the window and watching her. Then one day she was looking in a mirror and saw a strange-looking entity whose head appeared to rotate 360 degrees. Its eyes also seemed to move independently of each other. It finally got to the stage where Vera couldn't bear to be alone in her own home.

While Derek had not personally witnessed any of these events, he knew his wife well enough to know something was not right. He knew Vera had always been a little nervous of the unknown, but in their thirty-five years of marriage he had never seen her behave in the manner she had over the last six weeks. Derek knew Vera was more than nervous—he knew she was terrified—and that was good enough for him. If his wife said something was watching her, then he believed it to be true.

Vera learned about me and my skills through the Mind, Body, and Spirit shop in a local town. When she called, I admit I was rather intrigued by her story of becoming haunted after a visit by a psychic. I had heard of mediums removing lost souls but never of a ghost being deposited!

Lyn, Bill, Patrick, and I were joined by Rachel, an adept psychic and Reiki Master. On Easter bank holiday, which was a Monday, we met on the large driveway at Vera's. We hesitated for a few minutes, connecting and harmonizing ourselves before going to knock on the front door.

Vera and Derek lived in a large and spacious dormer-bungalow. The building seemed exceptionally large for just the two of them. They noted the home had been extensively refurbished and a first floor had been introduced three years ago. Indeed the interior was very nice. The polished oak staircase with its fancy balustrade was the central feature of the place. A large bedroom had been added to the floor, as well as a smaller room, a bathroom, and sizeable study. A big and ornate window set in the external wall added to the luster of the area.

Vera explained that the problem had started upstairs in the large study where the psychic had carried out her readings. We decided to walk around this ground floor and psychically scanned and delved for hidden, disembodied spirits and any other type of phenomena that may have been running amok. We suddenly felt compelled to go up to the first floor.

As we climbed the beautiful staircase I could feel the point where the energies of the disembodied spirit began to taint the ether of the home. On step number nine, the energies changed. We moved along and went from room to room and collectively decided that our starting point would be the large study.

Placing Vera and Derek in between us, we formed a large circle that encompassed the whole room. With the space sealed, we began to bring in walls of energy to the entire room so we could see what it was we were dealing with.

At first this male entity moved quickly from corner to corner as he did his best to avoid us. When he realized his efforts were futile, he decided to bluff his way out. He slowly and deliberately sauntered into the middle of the circle. Now we could see him clearly.

It was a man in his mid-thirties. He appeared to be at ease with the area, giving off the impression he had been a local, but that was not something we could ascertain. His clothing gave the impression he had most likely died within the last forty years. We could sense that he had no thought or consideration for Vera and, in fact, he appeared to be nothing more than a bully who enjoyed causing upset. He liked to remain hidden from Derek, preferring people he could control and frighten. He really wanted nothing to do with anyone who could challenge him and erode his power.

He started to throw his weight around, but when he moved towards Vera, Lyn blocked his way. He seemed to be a master of creeping up and startling people. This tactic was very good at producing the bolts of fear he thrived on. He moved away from Vera and came at me. I held my space and dared him to come closer. He hesitated and then moved away and went towards Rachel, who also dared him to approach her.

His efforts failing, he now began to crumble, because he had no one to attack and no way out. His hesitation was his downfall as we began to close the gap around him. No loving mother was going to entice him over because he had broken the spiritual laws and terrorized Vera. He would be removed the hard way.

The space where he stood became smaller and smaller. A gray doorway opened and unseen energies began to suck him through this tiny opening where he would find he had to take responsibility for his actions. He began to spin and turn as he sought a means of escape, but there was none, and within moments he was gone.

We then began to systematically move through the house, checking the other rooms for signs of unseen entities.

We swept through every room until we got to where there were the dogs of the house. We could feel their sadness at being unable to protect their mistress and their terror of this now-disposed entity, yet, we knew they had done their best to protect Vera despite their fear.

We also knew they were now happy dogs who knew the enemy had gone, never to return.

Be Careful Who You Let Help You

Regardless of their motives or good intentions, unless people know what they are doing, they can make a clearance situation ten times worse—and this next family found it out the hard way.

Rita lived with her husband, their youngest daughter and her family, and Poppy, the eldest granddaughter, who was twelve. Poppy was convinced there was something on the landing and it was waiting to get her. During the night, the child refused to go from her room to the bathroom unless someone accompanied her. Further, she refused to go up to her bedroom alone.

About six months after Poppy started having her feelings, all hell broke loose in the house and problems began to arise in all the rooms that could only be described as a ceaseless onslaught.

Whenever the families entered the living room, they argued with each other and afterwards couldn't remember how the argument had started. The living room was always dark and freezing cold with an energy that was anything but inviting.

In the daughter's bedroom, scratching sounds emitted from a cupboard and lasted for up to ten minutes. The scratching would cease as soon as the door was opened and would start up again when the door was closed. The mother had also been physically attacked by a giant featherless spirit bird and the baby granddaughter had been attacked as well. Doors would slam so hard that bits of plaster fell off the walls. Such was the tension in the house that both marriages were in jeopardy.

Driven by the desire to save her own relationship with her husband, Rita was desperate to try to improve the situation and decided to seek help.

Rita knew a friend of a friend who went to a healing at a church. The friend mentioned Rita's situation to Martin, who at the time was the healing leader at the church, and this in turn led Rita to me.

Martin and I, along with Karen and Paul, went to the property—but soon found out that we were not the first to be called in about the paranormal activity. A ghost hunting team had been there previously.

Rita reported the list of things that had been happening and noted that the center of activity appeared to be the living room, kitchen, and dining area. However, considering what had happened earlier with Poppy on the upstairs landing, we decided to keep our options open.

We went upstairs and down, and then repeated this. We now knew the problem definitely appeared to be around the living room and kitchen areas. The property had a very long landing that ran almost the width of the house upstairs. Karen and Martin picked up quickly on a gentleman in his late sixties dressed in clothing from the beginning of the twentieth century. He was moving from one property to another.

"Do you know what stood here before?" Martin asked. "It's just that I'm picking up an old man, and I don't think he lived here," he added.

"Mining connections," Karen added absentmindedly.

Rita nodded in agreement. "All around here was opencast mining before these properties were built, and there were some old houses over in the back."

Martin looked at me. "I don't think he is the problem," he said, meaning the spirit man.

I told Martin that I totally agreed with him.

"Rita, does the bathroom door ever open on its own?" I asked.

"All the time," she responded.

"And do you hear knocking from inside?" I queried.

Rita nodded her head in agreement. "This has gone on for years, ever since we moved in, although it has never bothered us."

"How long ago was that?" Paul asked.

"Around seven years ago. In fact, that was the only problem we ever had until about six months ago," Rita responded.

Yes, there was a spirit man here on the property and I suspected he had been here for a very long time—probably during the time of the previous owners as well. But this spirit did not appear to be the problem. No, there was something else here, and this entity was much more sinister. This was most likely a demon—something we had encountered many times before. Usually this type of situation was associated with a Ouija board.

I took a deep breath, because I had to ask. We couldn't move forward with anything until we had the answer. Knowing glances were passing between us.

"Rita, everything here is indicating that someone has probably been using something like a Ouija board in the house."

She jumped right in and was very emphatic. "No! Never! They all know better."

Now it became a little more difficult; White Feather was telling me a board or something similar had been used here. Whatever was on this property was not of this world and something had invited it in. A doorway had been opened, and we needed to close it.

I was just about to start in again when a look of realization came on Rita's face. "We haven't used a board, but the ghost investigators did!"

We could see the light coming on in her mind when she recalled how the ghost hunters had visited and used a board to talk to the unwanted guest.

Now we knew we were battling something from the lower astral plane, which had come here by invitation. Knowing what we were up against, we could begin the banishment.

While the living room was dreadful, the hub of the activity was in the kitchen. We walked around until we located the precise spot where we felt the veil between the dimensions had been ripped and the beast had flown in. Coincidentally, it was the exact point where the ghost hunters had used the makeshift Ouija board.

We began to manipulate the energy to tightly box in the area. We could all feel the angry, powerful, and icy cold energy around us that was totally devoid of love and emotion. This entity was well established here. It had been growing nicely and had no intention of going anywhere.

Fortunately, we only had to wait moments for the other side to come for the entity. We held the beast in a box of light and looked away while the other side pulled the entity through the veil, removing it to its rightful place. No sooner had it slipped through than the veil was re-sealed forever.

We did our final work of sealing the doorways and sent ripples or waves of positive energy through the rooms to shift any residual negative energies that might have been left or built up over a period of time. We used Mexican waves, with several of them running parallel with each other in a much tighter frequency, ensuring the energy penetrated every nook and cranny of the room.

In the meantime, the spirit man on the landing—who was clearly afraid of the entity that had just been banished—kept well out of the way. Not wanting to leave him trapped here, we turned our attentions to him. We gently brought his wife through to him and we watched as she led him by the hand through the silver doorway back to the place where he belonged.

Just before we left, Rita brought out a picture one of the ghost hunters had drawn during the investigation. They had told Rita the picture had been drawn by a baby she had lost. The picture was hideous and we told her to throw it away.

I am sure the ghost hunters who came to this house did not mean to cause the family any upset or anguish, and if they even had an inkling of the distress they had caused they would be mortified—but the truth of the matter was they did cause great trouble for this family, simply because they had no idea what they were doing.

Assistance from the Other Side

Carmel was convinced she was the victim of Voodoo, a form of black magic. She reported that many unusual and frightening things had been occurring in her home: her disabled son's bed had been dragged across the room with him asleep in it, photographs mysteriously disappeared from her albums and off the walls only to reappear at a later date, pages were ripped out of the family bible, and both Carmel and her daughter saw a large, hideous male figure on the landing.

The final straw for the family was the day they returned home and found a pile of shoes in the middle of the living room with their laces tied in perfect knots.

On a cold and damp November evening, Paul, Bill, Lyn, and I met on the street outside of Carmel's house. As with many modern estates, there was no space for vehicles, so we parked around the corner and walked. As we had rounded the corner, the house was directly in front of us. It was an end terrace with a high gable.

Paul was the first to speak. "Can you see the strange lighting around the house?" He pointed towards what he was seeing and we followed his gaze. We could clearly see what he was indicating and it looked most odd. It was as if there were several searchlights directed at the house. It was amazing! The whole gable end of the place was lit up with a golden beam of light and this light was almost bright enough to cause us to squint. We looked around for the source of this strange light but could see no street or security lights that could be causing it.

I must say that I know very little about the subject of Voodoo or black magic, but I am certain there are many people who do intentionally call up such dark forces—and I wondered if that could be the cause of what was going on here.

When we went into the house that night, we were confronted with something that was definitely not of this world.

Hiding in the back of a cupboard in Carmel's bedroom we found a small black ball of concentrated energy. The entity obviously felt quite safe and had secured a place where it could remain undetected—oddly enough, the light we had seen from the outside had been illuminating this spot!

Once we found the entity, our job was to try to pin it in one particular space and the other side would come and exile it to where it belonged.

I must say I have never seen anything move in the manner in which this thing did. As we tried to contain it, it moved at great speed and began to traverse the walls and ceiling. For several minutes we chased it from room to room as it darted around. It tried every maneuver possible as it hid in corners, behind the television, and underneath things in an attempt to get away from us.

We realized this darkness had been conjured up and had been brought into this world with a task to perform and it wasn't going to leave until it had fulfilled its duty. This was a curse in motion. I could feel its power and knew none of us was a match for it. Then, in my mind's eye, I saw White Feather's hand rise up in warning. He was telling me not to communicate with the entity because if I did there would be a risk of shifting the course of the curse to myself. I didn't need to be told twice and instructed the others not to communicate with this thing.

The entity kept darting around the room and evading our attempts to catch it. We created walls of silver light, encasing the whole of the room. We raised the floors, lowered the ceiling, and brought the walls in until we had it boxed in a very small space. We finally managed to pin it down and as soon as we did the other side leapt into action. We provided the power to the earth link that allowed the ethereal world to pull this vibration from our dimension and return it to its own. After about twenty minutes of chasing the entity from room to room, we were finally able to capture it.

When the entity was gone, we scanned through the house, but there was nothing further to clear—no dark vibrations remained—all the evil had been contained in this one dark ball.

As we said our goodbyes and left a much calmer Carmel behind, we were thankful that the other side had given us a clue by showing us the light around the precise spot where the fiend had been hidden.

Four

Tales of Possession

One of the absolutely most horrific things to witness is a true demonic possession, which is the taking over of an individual by a malevolent entity. Before your eyes the person changes into something totally evil, vile, and frightening. Here are a few of the cases our group has dealt with.

Money Stolen by a Ghost

Valerie's experiences had spanned several years, coincidentally beginning around the time she had begun to train in crystal healing therapy. As she had practiced her newly learned skills, she became aware of a guardian angel. Over the next year or so, she developed a strong relationship with this angel who called himself Raphael. Valerie believed with all her heart that this angel was a messenger from God, and so she welcomed his presence in her life.

Then, over the last few months, the relationship with Raphael began to take a more sinister turn and the requests he made of her became incredibly bizarre. This had her believing the angel was not who he claimed to be. As the realization began to grow, she felt at a total loss as to how to deal with this or who to turn to.

Valerie confessed that fifteen years previously she had suffered from a breakdown in her mental health. She felt unable to go to her doctor to discuss a voice she had recently been hearing in her head, because she was convinced the doctor would think she was having a further episode of mental illness. This inability to confide in anyone only served to delay her quest for help.

Further, at the request of her "angel," she had told no one of his existence. Then one day she decided to confide in her crystal healing teacher, and this in turn led Val to me.

On the advice of this angel Val had given away a large amount of money. The sizable settlement she had received for her divorce was now all gone, because the Raphael angel had convinced her that in order to receive more money she had to give it away. On one occasion, the angel told her she had won the lottery. Next he persuaded her to start drinking alcohol, telling her this was a means for her to reach the Lord. Raphael also encouraged her to self-pleasure in preparation for receiving the Lord. One day she found herself intoxicated and lying naked on the bed. That was the final straw.

When Paul, Lyn, Bill, and I arrived at the house, a very nervous Val invited us in and told us more about her ordeal. While she talked, we noticed many writing pads everywhere. These were found to be filled with rambling sentences the angel had channeled through her. After reading some of the writing, I gently pointed out that the words written made no sense at all. I asked Val to share some of the revelations Raphael had promised to give her. Val stared at me blankly for a few minutes and then rather hesitantly said, "There aren't any, are there?" I was afraid I had to agree with her.

Val was bewildered and angry, but when I asked her if she wanted this angel removed, she emphatically stated that she did. I truly believed at this point this kind and gentle woman would have gladly punched the thing on the nose for all the pain it had caused.

We sat Val in the kitchen, the widest space possible. Paul was working from behind, Lyn was to my left, and Bill to my right. We asked Val to trust us and follow what we said. I explained to her we were going to try to persuade this disembodied spirit to leave voluntarily, but if he would not, our guides would encourage him to do so. The entity was already boxed in to a very small space and going nowhere. It could now only come forward and try to defeat us.

I asked Val to allow me to talk to her angel.

"He's not here," Val said in a muffled tone as her chin rested on her chest.

"Yes he is," I said. Then I added, "Do you think he is afraid of me?"

Silence.

"Does he think we are too powerful for him?" I asked, prodding for a response.

This challenge was too much for Raphael. Val raised her head and lifted her chin to emphasize the entity's contempt for me.

Val grimaced, and the eyes and face I was seeing were no longer hers. Through Val, this entity looked directly into my eyes, and I immediately felt a surge of power shoot out from Val's energetic field and hit me in the solar plexus as the entity tried to displace me. It felt as if I had been kicked in the stomach; it hurt badly. While I was feeling somewhat unnerved, I betrayed no emotion in my demeanor.

Realizing it had not had the desired effect on me, the entity again lowered Val's chin down to rest on her chest. I knew the fake angel was only resting while plotting its next move, and we didn't have long. Before Val could have a chance to snatch her own body back, the entity leapt into action! It surged her out of the chair and, with bared teeth and wild eyes, Val shot forward as if she were going to lunge at me!

Within seconds Lyn and Bill stepped forward and placed their hands on Val's shoulders. With total command, Lyn told the entity to return to the chair and stay seated. With Val now back on the seat, I was confident the risk of attack had passed. Lyn and Bill moved back to Val's sides and allowed me full visual contact with Val.

Suddenly Val changed completely and began to speak in tongues! Not one word of English could be deciphered from her utterances. Her wild eyes appeared to move independently of one another, much like those of a lizard, and a snarling face spat out incomprehensible words. With each rant, Val displayed bared teeth and a contorted and twisted face. Then, as quickly as it began, this display stopped and Val fell back on the chair.

The entity went very quiet for a moment before again lifting its head and locking its eyes with mine. Val's eyes and jaw protruded. Again it lunged at me and again Bill and Lyn pinned it down. The strength Val showed that night was not of a woman in her late fifties, and Lyn and Bill had to use all their strength to keep Val on the chair. Of course Bill and Lyn had the upper hand in terms of positioning, yet at times they struggled mightily to maintain her in a seated position.

Realizing it was losing the battle, the entity sat still for a moment and then again began to speak in tongues. This display was completely different from the first rant, because distinct vowels could be made out, but it was still not a language of our world. As it spoke, it spat out the words through clenched teeth. In between words, Val's chin jutted forward in an aggressive manner and the entity glared at me from her eyes. Then the ranting went quiet, but the entity still maintained eye contact with me. I looked directly back into its eyes and then moved closer to it and in a raised voice simply said one word. "Boo!"

This single word shot out of my mouth and was delivered with a ferocity that was meant to frighten. It had the desired effect. The wild-eyed Val was able to physically pull back as my response had unnerved the entity. This was not at all the sort of retaliation it had expected, and the momentary faltering on the entity's part was enough to make it push back and further loosen its hold on Val. This was the fatal flaw in the fraudulent angel's makeup. The fiend cleared Val's throat and threw her head backwards and then pushed her head forward. I knew its intention was to spit directly into my face, yet I refused to move. I continued to glare back at this being and willed it to spit at me. My whole persona challenged it and I almost shouted aloud, "Bring it on! Join battle!" because I knew this was a battle I had to win for Val's sake.

At the last moment, the entity's nerve failed and instead it spat on the floor to the side of me. One unexpected "boo" had been enough to shake it up, and it was beginning to weaken. It fell back into silence and Val was now back in control.

"Do you want this entity to leave?" I asked.

"Yes! Get rid of it now please!" she answered.

With her permission we began the final act. Within a few moments, a doorway opened and an unseen force slowly pulled the entity through the gateway. It was kicking and screaming as it was dragged from our world back to where it belonged. When the incident ended that night, not a scrap of the disembodied spirit remained in this dimension.

Val, on the other hand, would take a long time to overcome the pain and trauma the entity had caused her. The violation visited upon her would remain with her for quite a long time. But there were other repercussions: the money she had was gone and could not be gotten back; worse than that, Val was left with the shame and humiliation that she had been duped by a dark force into believing that she was indeed working with an angel for the good of God and this planet.

For several days after this event, Val was extremely worried and called to tell me the entity was trying to communicate with her. I told her to refuse to acknowledge it or even think about it. And I have to say there were times when all of us in the group doubted Val would have the strength to keep the entity at bay—but she did.

I often wondered, as many would—why Val? What had she done to attract this entity? The answer is she had done nothing at all. What I believe is that Val was in the wrong place at the wrong time. The entity might have heard her talking about angels and about how much she loved them and simply decided to try its luck. It had probably listened closely to what Val had said about angels to others and repeated back what it had heard her saying. This would have been all she needed to convince herself that an angel was communicating with her.

Who Is the Weakest Link?

As is often the case, Danny was pretty desperate by the time she found us. Things had been going on in her house for about three years—from incidents that could be viewed as a little strange all the way to something nightmarish. An attack on her daughter by an unseen force had left her feeling helpless because she was unable to protect her child.

Now the activity was increasing in frequency and Danny's nineteen-year-old daughter Becky was afraid to sleep in her bedroom. She had been waking up frequently with the strong sense that someone was standing over her—a "darkness," as Becky described it. This thing often came so close, the child could almost feel its breath on her face. Other times she would awaken with the sensation that something was lying on top of her. Such was the force pressing her down that she would find herself unable to move and barely able to breathe. On other occasions, she had been pulled from her bed and dragged by her feet towards the window, and her body had been banged into the wardrobes in the process. She would then be thrown from one side of the room to the other and then back onto her bed.

There had also been several incidents when Becky had collapsed on the landing and appeared to suffer from some kind of fit. Her eyes would roll back in her head and she appeared to have no control over her body. Extensive neurological tests had been done and proved inconclusive, so there was no medical reason for what Becky was experiencing.

There was also an episode that had occurred on the stairs, and it was noted that Becky had been very lucky not to suffer a serious fall.

From all of this information, it was easy to see Becky was the focus of the majority of the paranormal activity in the house.

Danny had also visited with two clergymen at different times when she was seeking help. Both had come and blessed the house, but even that did not stop the onslaught. A black shadow was seen standing under the stairs watching people as they walked by. Sometimes the shadow would be halfway down the stairs towards the bottom and would peep around the balustrade. Even the grandmother had seen a scruffy-looking, dark-haired man standing perfectly still in the same spot.

Lyn, Bill, Paul, Rachel and I arrived at the property at 9:00 p.m. We proceeded to the fairly modern traditional semi-house that had clearly been extended and was very well-maintained.

We gathered in the living room and spent some time talking to Danny and the grandmother. We had to do further fact-finding to establish a clearer picture of what we were up against. As the house was already sealed from the outside, there was no rush.

After a few minutes, it became apparent that Danny had been drinking. She was not falling over, but her speech was slightly slurred—and this put us in a dilemma. If we postponed our visit, the entity was liable to increase the frequency or intensity of the onslaughts against Becky. It was imperative that everyone present have their wits about them, and Danny's drinking would have a definite impact.

We reluctantly decided to proceed for Becky's sake and promptly made our way to her bedroom.

Despite the tiger-print wallpaper, matching white pine furniture, contrasting curtains and duvet cover, the room was dark and the atmosphere oppressive. It was almost impossible to penetrate this foreboding darkness, and it was as if we hadn't entered the room at all. We began to scan the room in order to ascertain what was troubling the family, and then we strategically placed Danny, Becky, and the grandmother in the middle of our circle as we continued our search. A few minutes later, Danny went to sit on the bed.

Suddenly Danny cried out that she couldn't breathe. Indeed her breathing was becoming erratic and she grabbed frantically at her chest, as if trying to pull off some unseen force.

The panic rose in her voice. "Help me!" she screamed. "Help me! I can't breathe! There's something on my chest! Oh God!" At this, Danny fell back on the bed and began twisting and writhing as she fought with this unseen force.

It took only seconds for us to realize what had happened. This had to be a ploy by the entity to divert our attention. Simultaneously, Lyn and Bill leapt into action.

"Come on, Danny. It's fine. Just breathe," Lyn said in a soothing voice. But this fell on deaf ears as Danny continued to gasp for breath and writhe about. Bill, Rachel, and I chimed in, calmly telling Danny to breathe.

Suddenly, quiet fell in the room as Danny appeared to stop breathing altogether.

A piercing scream came from Becky. "Mom! Breathe! Please!"

Becky's plea brought Danny back. Coughing and sputtering, she began to take deep breaths. Her face was quite red and her neck and chest were equally red, as if this force had been there doing harm.

A few moments later, Danny appeared to have recovered. She threw her head forward and opened her eyes. But things were not at all normal; in fact, they were horribly altered.

Danny's warm, brown eyes were now replaced by blood-red ones. The confirmed Christian, who attended church on a regular basis, had changed in an instant! She had switched from a loving mother and wife to someone who was possessed!

All hell broke loose as Danny began to spit, scream, swear, kick, and punch at anyone she could make contact with. She yelled out profanities and screamed at each of us in turn.

We quickly worked, using every technique we could muster to free this dark entity from Danny's energy field.

When we finally got a look at it, the beast appeared to be at least six feet tall, and then it compressed itself down to two feet. It was locked in and here to stay. It knew exactly what it was doing and also knew the alcohol had rendered Danny unable to fight it off. Each time we removed it from Danny, it simply jumped back on again. The situation was feeling very hopeless.

We had no choice, so we created a diversion. We stopped our efforts for a moment. Lyn looked across at me and I then saw what she was doing; Lyn had opened her energy and offered herself as prey.

For the entity, the challenge was too much and it rose from Danny and moved across onto Lyn—but it still maintained a foothold on Danny while it did this.

In a scene fit for any horror movie, Danny switched from a screaming fiend back to herself. Danny was in a state of utter bewilderment as, with a tearful voice, she inquired about what was happening to her. Seconds later, she was back to screaming as the demon overpowered her again.

Throughout this process, Becky called out to her mother, telling her how much she loved her and begging her to stop. Also during this whole time, the grandmother kept a comforting arm around Becky's shoulders as she also called out to Danny to take control.

Lyn let her guard down and invited this entity to take over her body, because she knew she had the power with our help to throw it off. The demon knew Lyn was a greater challenge, but Danny, impaired by alcohol, was a sure bet. So the entity moved backwards and forwards. Such was its power, it was able to enter into Lyn's energy field, yet still maintain a hold on Danny.

Rachel moved in to help Danny while Bill and I took the demon to task.

The battle was now on to shift this monster from Lyn. Lyn raised her head and we saw that her soft, brown eyes were gone and now replaced by coal-black ones that beamed hatred at me. Such was the power that poured from Lyn as this demon tried to instill fear and terror in me as it battled to overtake her. I knew this was one battle the demon would not win, because Lyn had such great power and strength. She had lured the fiend in with false promises of her weakness and servitude, and now it was to realize the true power of Lyn.

As the entity locked eyes with me, Lyn held it in abeyance through her own power. Suddenly the spirit guides came to me and told me to tell Lyn several jokes. Without question, I did as they instructed and soon Lyn started to laugh, and this laughter spread through her whole body. The guides knew exactly what they were doing—they knew that laughter, being an alien vibration to the demon, would weaken its hold on Lyn. Confused by the laughter, the demon began to weaken.

Instantly Bill and Paul sent power from the sides. They removed the entity by knocking it through a portal and back to the world from which it came.

Residual energy continued to have a hold on Danny and a further battle ensued. She moved from violent outbursts to lucid moments when she would ask in a still-bewildered voice about what was happening. And then in a flash the dark energy would take hold of her again. We eventually managed to push that residual energy away from her, and when at last it was over, Danny was back.

The bedroom was now clear and the vibration changed as a bright light appeared to replace the darkness that had so recently existed there. The arrival of the light was all the indication we needed to know that everything was truly back to normal.

We moved on to check the remaining rooms of the house and came to the spot under the stairs that also seemed to be a center of activity. Here we found a huge vortex that ran vertically through the house and straight through Becky's bedroom, into the loft conversion, and stretched many feet above the house. This vortex was the doorway by which the demon had managed to enter the property—and the demon had not come alone. During the course of this evening we found a total of four small entities and an incubus (a male demon believed to have sex with sleeping females). By the time the property was cleared the house felt like it had undergone an energy makeover.

The next day, Danny reported that Becky had said their home felt clear, fresh, and vibrant, and everyone could feel the difference.

The summary of that evening was clear. Danny or another member of the family had somehow revealed our intention in the presence of the demon. Realizing its demise was near, it had impressed upon Danny that she should drink alcohol. In truth, this was an incredibly powerful beast, capable of using mind control by telling Danny that drinking was good. This intelligent demon did not think we could defeat it if Danny remained inebriated—and it had viewed Danny as the weakest link. It knew the focus would be on Becky, so by possessing the mother it created a diversion, believing that it would be almost impossible to remove. Someone who is drunk is unable to assist in this type of situation and their cooperation is imperative in the process of cleansing an aura. The demon knew this and used it to its own advantage. Fortunately, on this occasion we won.

It took Lyn two days to recover from this experience.

A Very, Very Powerful Demon

Something told me this was not going to be an easy call.

I listened intently as Dominic's mom Sue told me their story, and as she spoke I realized we had a huge problem on our hands.

Dominic's trouble had begun very suddenly about eight weeks prior. He had been at his girlfriend's with a couple of his friends and their girlfriends and they had smoked some cannabis—a drug that allows some people to mentally wander into other dimensions. Dominic was a typical eighteen-year-old who portrayed that he knew more than most adults ever could, but underneath all this bravado was a very sensitive soul. Dominic had told his mother on several occasions that he did not like the atmosphere in his girlfriend's house, although he admitted he couldn't pinpoint exactly why.

Dominic had spoken to his mother about a cupboard in the home that seemed to house something evil. Apparently one day the door of the cupboard opened and something rushed at him as if it wanted to get into his body. That same night, unable to sleep, he had watched something with red eyes enter in through his eyes. From this point on, the boy's behavior changed radically and he would fly into violent rages and roar like an animal. On these occasions, it would take up to eight people to hold him down.

There had been no help for Dominic until a friend of a friend recommended me.

We did not want this demon to take Dominic away from us, so Bill, Lyn, Paul, and I arrived unannounced and immediately began working before the demonic force had a chance to try anything.

We sat Dominic down and explained to him what we were going to do. When we asked if he wanted the demon removed, he nodded with the usual enthusiasm expected from a teenager. Just to make sure, I asked him again, and he stated that he did want us to help him. With Dominic's permission secured, we began to position ourselves, strategically channeling the energy. Lyn was to the left, Bill to the right, and I directly in front of the boy. Paul was standing behind me, pushing energy from behind, both through me and around me.

"Dominic, will you do one thing for me?" I asked.

"Yes," he said.

"You are going to fly at me and try to attack me, because whatever is with you knows I am the controlling force. It will try, through you, to stop me. Do you understand this?" I asked.

Dominic nodded that he understood.

"Will you sit on your hands, and no matter what happens will you promise to not let go of the backs of your legs?"

"I promise," he said.

I prompted him and he did as instructed. We would soon find it was probably this one act that saved us both. With everything in place we began.

Almost immediately, this entity came forward and Dominic let out a mighty roar. It was almost as if fangs appeared in his mouth. His head moved in strange motions as the roaring continued. For most of this time, Dominic's eyes remained shut; it was as though this beast had no need to use eyes. When Dominic's eyes finally opened, they were far from being the soft, brown eyes of a teenager—these eyes were glazed, unfocused, and dark in color. The boy bent over and lowered his chest down so it was pressed onto his lap. He was held firmly in position by Lyn and Bill, who applied a constant downward force on Dominic's shoulders.

In order to try to loosen the demon's hold, we initially bombarded Dominic with huge amounts of white light in an effort to displace this beast. As we did, the boy's body would writhe and contort as strange animalistic sounds emitted from his mouth. Occasionally the beast would try to hide, offering us hope that it had left. Fortunately, a mother's love cannot be fooled; Sue would move closer to her son and look at his face and immediately tell us, "That is not Dominic!"

And so we would begin again.

I can honestly say that for the first time in my career of doing this work I felt defeated and deflated. But one glance at this young man and his mother was enough to keep me going forward. Every time I glanced at the team, I knew they felt the same way and that we could not abandon this family. So we went on.

We continued to bombard the entity and blast it with light. We had to weaken it in order for our guides to do their work. Rays of hope began to penetrate the gloom. We felt it was losing its grip on the boy, because now, instead of being in the whole of his body, it had moved to key parts; Dominic was able to show us where it was. Finally, little by little, we were beginning to win. We could begin to focus our efforts on the points he was giving us.

"It's in my stomach! It's in my stomach!" Dominic repeated. He then grimaced and writhed as if in extreme pain. "God it's killing me!" he said during a lucid moment. We began to loosen the demon's hold on Dominic's solar plexus, but a battle ensued at each one of the power points, or chakras, in the boy's body. This whole process was interspersed with Dominic attempting to get up and physically attack me.

By now we were all exhausted, but to disengage from the situation would have been fatal.

I tuned into the guides; I knew they could feel our hopelessness and despair, and they urged us to bombard the demon with love. With fresh enthusiasm I re-engaged and, turning to the team, I urged them to switch to a love vibration. I also told Sue to visualize covering her son in love. Quickly we all began covering Dominic with loving thoughts and energy. We called his name in a loving way and expressed our love for him.

This was not a vibration the demon understood. In his realm of being, this vibration was alien. All this love began to unnerve the beast, and we continued on because we had the greatest love of all—that of the other side. Slowly we gained a bit of victory.

Realizing it was losing the battle, the demon somehow managed to get Dominic's hands free. The boy clenched at his throat and was now beginning to crush his own windpipe! Dominic cried and writhed as he gasped for breath.

This attack by the demon was sudden, relentless, and vicious. It was only the efforts of Lyn and Bill that stopped this entity from doing more damage to the boy. Such was the brutality of the attack that bruises appeared instantly on Dominic's throat. We paused for a moment to allow Dominic to get his breath back to a semblance of normal.

"How are you?" I asked.

In short, sharp gasps of air he nodded his head. "I'm okay," he said hoarsely.

"Are you sure?" I asked with great concern and uncertainty in my voice.

"Yes," he replied. "Carry on."

As we continued I couldn't help but feel great admiration for this boy's strength—not many adults could have withstood what Dominic did that night.

This last attack on Dominic was the beginning of the end for the demon. We had loosened his hold on the boy. Now the other side was able to perform their work. As the fiend began to leave I watched as a gigantic black liquid millipede poured from Dominic's body into a black hole directly behind him. This entity was huge and it seemed impossible that something this size could be contained in a human body. Indeed, the departure of this beast seemed to take forever, but in reality it was only a few minutes.

Dominic's energy field now needed to be cleansed and the holes the demon had created had to be filled. Instantaneously we all felt a higher being joining its energy with Dominic's. We could all see a tall female angel descend down to the boy. The aura of this being was pure golden. She had white, pointed wings and she was very beautiful. We watched as she slowly merged her aura with Dominic's, and they both became one as this final cleansing began. Such was the damage done to his aura that he needed a power far greater than anything we could provide to put him right.

But we were to find that even after the demon was gone and Dominic's aura righted, he still appeared strange—not in a dark way any longer—but through the gaining of a new skill.

Dominic was now incredibly psychic.

Dominic turned to Bill and asked. "Who was Jill?"

Bill never flinched at the question, but it must have shocked him, because Jill was the name of his mother, who had died quite recently. It should be noted that Dominic had no prior knowledge of Bill or his family.

Dominic then went on to speak about the angel the spirit world had sent down to him. He described her in great detail, speaking of her golden robes and pure white wings. Then he sat talking to her for a short while—clearly in deep conversation. We could only hear Dominic's side of the conversation at this point, but afterwards he explained to us that the angel said she would stay with him and look after him for as long as he needed her.

We decided to check on Dominic's bedroom. He wanted to stay behind and he requested that Lyn stay with him.

The energy in the bedroom was dark. As we walked into the room, it was as if we had actually penetrated the atmosphere. A sensation of discomfort poured through the whole area, and we all felt as if eyes were watching our every move. Despite this, we were unable to determine the location of where the eyes may actually have been peering at us. I left Paul and Bill to cleanse the room and went downstairs.

When I returned to Dominic and Lyn, Dominic told me to go back upstairs. He said the demon was hanging around by his bed and that a Dark Reaper had come to fetch it, but it needed my help to push it through the doorway. I immediately went back upstairs.

As I walked into the room, Bill pointed to a space by the window and said he felt that there was something still here—something not quite right.

I needed no more prompting. With the help of Bill and Paul, we pushed the final remnants of the beast out through the doorway to the Dark Reaper.

I went back downstairs and told Dominic and Lyn what had happened. I then explained to Dominic the importance of refusing to acknowledge this demon again. I told him to ignore it and, no matter how tempting it was, to refuse to communicate with it. I further explained he was right about the angel. She would stay with him for as long as he needed her and she would guard the doorway to his soul.

I also suggested he place an imaginary mirror over his stomach to protect himself. With great innocence he looked at me and asked how he would get out at night if he covered this area. This remark was indicative, not of remaining trouble, but of his latent psychic talent. We all leave our bodies during our sleep state where we travel the astral plane or return home. We remain attached to our bodies through a silver cord. The solar plexus is an energy portal and is important for our departure and return. Dominic was advanced enough to know if he capped this energy portal there was a real risk this would stop him from travelling, and he was afraid he would be trapped here forever. I looked at him and smiled, confident that we had finally removed this demon force from his energetic field.

We left the property at about 10 p.m. and went out for a quick drink together just to be in one another's company. We sat reflecting about the events that had unfolded this night. We were physically, spiritually, mentally, and emotionally exhausted. This was the closest we had ever come to losing a battle.

We didn't stay long and soon set off on our way. As I got into the car I glanced down at the clock and it read 11:33 p.m. This meant we had been in the restaurant for ninety minutes. That was impossible; we only had a drink or two and weren't in the restaurant for long. I could only conclude that all four of us had somehow slipped into a different time for a short period so that we could be restored and receive cleansing to ensure none of this darkness was attached to us.

Overpowered by Darkness

One evening my teaching session at the spiritualist church was disturbed by the incessant ringing of the telephone.

The call was from a frantic member of the congregation, and it would seem something horrible had happened the day before that had totally frightened her.

Barbara explained to me that her daughter Abbie had banged her head during a drunken episode the previous evening. When Abbie came to, she appeared to Barbara to be possessed. In a deep and strange voice, Abbie told Barbara how her grandmother had born a bastard child while granddad was away at war. A dreadful argument had ensued and the grandfather had tried to kill the lover with his army-issued handgun. In the fracas, the lover had been shot and wounded, but not fatally. The grandfather loved his wife very much and when the child was born it was brought up as his own. Over time, memories had faded and the event was never mentioned again.

Barbara was dumbstruck! She was the only living person with the knowledge of that event—not even her husband was aware of it—and here was a twenty-three-year-old repeating the story word for word. This incident convinced Barbara something was terribly amiss with Abbie, however, the next day the daughter returned to her normal self.

I felt there was an entity very close to Abbie and this is where the information had come from. The seriousness of this call warranted me requesting of Barbara that she not tell Abbie of our impending visit so that no warning would be given to the demon. We arrived at the home un-announced.

When we got there, Abbie was surprised by our presence yet she was welcoming. This was all I needed. Paul, Karen, Martin, and I assembled together in the oblong open-plan kitchen with Barbara and Abbie. As we began to talk to Barbara and Abbie about this most recent event, Abbie told us the story of how she had, at the age of eight, been totally terrified of the dentist. During a treatment, she had been sedated and felt she had floated up out of her body and had watched the whole procedure. She said she could see everything that was happening to her, although she felt no pain. After this event, she had felt very different—as if something or someone had been with her from this point on and that whatever had joined with her had been dormant. Up until recently, Abbie had completely forgotten about the whole thing.

Abbie then told us that after her alcohol-fueled night she had returned home. Somehow she had managed to fall off the settee, banging her head in the process. What happened next reminded her of the trip to the dentist and now she felt these two incidents were related—but she had no idea how that could be. Yet, the similarities between the dentist visit and the drunken fall could not be denied. In both instances she could hear and see what was happening to her, but it was as if she were observing the event rather than participating in it. She said she could hear herself speaking, yet she had no control over what she was saying.

Barbara added that Abbie's face had been contorting and her eyes seemed glazed over. Barbara didn't know exactly how or why it had happened, but she believed someone or something had taken over her daughter.

Abbie went on to say she had awakened the next morning to see writing on her hand and writing all over the walls of her bedroom. Yet, there were no pens found in the bedroom. To have done this herself, she would have had to go downstairs, fetch a pen, and then take it back. Abbie had a partner who was adamant that Abbie had not gotten out of bed at all during the night.

We looked closely at the writing; it was small and neat and consisted of pleas for help. It was scrawled over several walls in the room and looked like it would have taken many hours to complete.

As I listened to Abbie, I looked at my team members and suddenly felt we were totally unconnected with one another. Each one was doing his or her own thing. Martin was tuning into Abbie's energy field, Karen was scanning Abbie's aura, and Paul was doing a combination of the two. We needed to regroup the team; when we work, it is extremely important that we function as one. On any case, we need to operate unilaterally, because if an entity tries to overpower us, we are all aware of it and pitch our energies together. When we are fragmented, we are vulnerable.

With the team now together, we decided to try to communicate with the entity and see if we could entice it out so we could break it away from Abbie.

We placed Abbie in the middle of the room. After a few moments Abbie wanted to get up and fetch her cardigan that was located in another area of the house. It was clear to us the entity was impressing to Abbie the need to get away from us. Thinking quickly, Martin handed Abbie Karen's coat, and Abbie placed this over her shoulders.

I said to Abbie, "You know he is trying to get you out of the room."

Abbie smiled. "I think he is." She settled back on a chair.

I knew that as long as we could show Abbie this being was the discarnate spirit trying to trick her to leave the room, she would remain calm. We knew Abbie wanted this thing gone and that would work in our favor.

I explained to Abbie that she was safe and we were there to protect her, but I really wanted to speak to the other being. I asked Abbie to let him through. We all did our best to cajole her, but it was clear that Abbie was afraid. Since we weren't having any success with the direct approach, we changed tactics.

"Abbie, tell us what he is saying," I said.

"Not sure," came the reply.

"Say the words," Martin urged.

All this time the blonde, blue-eyed beauty looked down at the ground.

Then she began to repeat the words. "'Bitch.' He is saying 'bitch,'" she said. Her eyes averted from mine.

"Is this me he is referring to?" I asked.

"Yes," Abbie replied with an edge to her voice.

This time Abbie looked directly into my eyes. As soon as she did this, I felt the power of the entity and I began to sway backwards.

Before I could speak Karen said, "It wants you out of the way, Sandrea. It's trying to push you against the wall."

I could feel it pushing me as I began to sway more and more to the point where I had to adjust my feet just to remain upright.

During this entire time Abbie's now-dark eyes stayed locked on mine. Abbie had now taken on a very confident persona, and it was going to be a battle of wills between the demon and me.

Quite suddenly I felt a huge surge of energy sweep through my body. This energy moved from my head to my toes and down the sides of my legs and arms. No sooner had this power entered my energy field when I felt it exit through my eyes and into Abbie's. I knew then that White Feather and another guide, White Cloud, were working together—using my aura to push through more power than this entity could generate. In doing so, the balance of power shifted. There was no need for me to do anything other than to hold Abbie's gaze as my guides went head-to-head with the dark force. At the same time, Karen, Martin, and Paul poured healing vibrations through Abbie's energetic field. As the battle ensued, Martin began to talk about seeing the being standing behind Abbie. He could feel and sense a dark and foreboding presence there. A few more choice words poured from Abbie's mouth and power continued to surge through me.

The others could clearly see the disembodied soul now. The light illuminating Abbie's auric field revealed his location. Now there was no hiding place for the entity. I continued to hold eye contact while Karen, Martin, and Paul began the process of removing this thing off Abbie's back. I looked at Abbie, and all the time her dark eyes glared at me. The thing on Abbie appeared to us all as a limpet or abnormal hump. Of course we were very careful when we were describing it so as not to frighten Abbie.

"Do you want this entity to leave?" Martin asked.

"Yes I do," Abbie stated very clearly and firmly.

We had located the entity, and we had Abbie's permission, so the process began.

Paul provided the power, Martin the healing, and Karen the guidance while I held Abbie's vibration. Among the three of them they slowly pushed the demon through a doorway they had created behind her.

"He is very reluctant to go," Karen said.

This reluctance on the demon's part only caused the team to push him harder. They struggled for several minutes until the entity was finally through the door.

I realized our mission was complete when Abbie broke eye contact and reverted back to her own persona—that of a shy young woman.

Our next task was to find the soul who had written on Abbie's hands and the wall. Almost instantly we found a young girl of about thirteen or fourteen. We all felt she had died quite suddenly. Her parents appeared and getting her to leave with them required nothing at all from us; in a moment she was gone.

All that was now required was to fill the hole in Abbie's aura with healing light, and this we duly did. Afterwards we asked Abbie how she felt and her response was, "Kinda odd. I almost feel lighter, if you can understand."

Of course we fully understood what she meant and we smiled at her and nodded in agreement. What had transpired with Abbie and how had it happened? I believe the entity had definitely become entangled in her aura during the dental visit and this is where it had stayed until the alcohol-fueled night revealed its existence.

Crossed by Darkness

I had known Eddie for many years and when she heard of the plight of an acquaintance, she immediately contacted me. According to Eddie, her friend Linda and daughter

Gemma had been plagued by strange occurrences ever since moving into their new home. The incidents had started with various banging and knocking sounds and progressed to the sensation of them both being pinned on a violently shaking bed. When a local shaman threw some salt down, the word "HELP" appeared, along with an arrow pointing to the adjacent property.

The day Eddie called me, she said she had seen Linda and felt she was behaving in a very strange manner—Linda's eyes were glazed, unfocused, and distant, and her voice was unrecognizable.

Bill, Lyn, Paul, and I arrived on a bleak February night. The rain was pouring down and the temperature barely above freezing, but despite the terrible weather conditions we quickly aligned our vibrations and ran to Linda's house. Once inside we found that the temperature was no better than it was outside. In the living room I glanced towards the gas fire and noted that every burner was ablaze. Then I walked over to the radiator and casually placed my hand on it; it was extremely warm. Despite all of this heat, none of it seemed to be penetrating the rest of the house. The lighting in the room was also subdued. Despite the fact there was a lamp on in the corner and the ceiling light was on, the light did not appear to penetrate the dark atmosphere that was present.

We spent time with Linda, but as we didn't know her very well it was difficult for us to ascertain if she was behaving any differently than usual. Her daughter did remark in front of Linda that she was extremely worried about Linda and, yes, her mother had been behaving strangely.

Linda explained to us that a few nights previous she had woken to the sensation that something was physically entering her body through her chest and stomach and had become part of her. She told of missing time frames and how her legs seemed to be trying to run in front of fast-moving traffic.

I decided it would be a good idea to have Linda remain on the settee while we checked out her aura to see what might be present. We placed ourselves at four key points all the way around her. Bill was behind at her head, Lyn and Paul opposite each other in line with her torso, and I was positioned in front of her feet. No sooner had we done this when all hell broke loose.

Linda threw her head back and arched her back while her eyes rolled back in her head. At the same time, she began writhing and contorting and uttered low moans that were interjected with cries for help. Her body moved and bounced around the settee as if she were suffering from some violent convulsion. After a few seconds the movements increased and we could see that Linda had no control of her body. Her daughter looked on in utter horror and seemed struck dumb by the whole episode.

As Linda writhed, she slipped off the sofa and onto the floor. As this motion continued, she began to move past me as her back and hips arched and contorted. I stood and watched in amazement.

Suddenly Bill called out to me, "Sandrea! She's getting away! Look!" he said, pointing to Linda. "She's breaking away from the circle!"

I sprang into action and placed my foot, side on, in front of her feet, blocking her from exiting the circle. As soon as I did, Linda's movements stopped instantly as the entity that had taken her over realized it had failed.

Standing unsteadily, Linda and her daughter, who were both badly shaken by the event, agreed with great trepidation to follow our request that they go upstairs. They really didn't want to return to the bedroom and risk the shaking of the bed and the pressure on their bodies starting again, and this was understandable. Unfortunately we had no choice, because we needed to flush the entity out. The two nodded at one another and then, holding hands, began to ascend up the stairs.

Linda and Gemma both got on the bed and we waited to see what was going to happen.

Almost immediately Linda began to complain of immense pressure on her chest and a feeling of being unable to breathe. "Help me! Help me!" she cried. "Get it off me! I can't breathe!"

Linda pulled frantically at her chest with both hands, as if trying to pull off some unseen force. As she writhed around the bed, Gemma was clearly terrified, and yet despite her fear she kept her voice calm and offered words of comfort to her mother.

The spirit world leapt into action and began the process of removing the entity off Linda, but not before it appeared to attack her throat. She screamed again, "Help me!" as she choked. "I can't breathe!" Linda's face was becoming redder and redder. We all offered support to her, as did Gemma, who stayed with Linda, holding her and stroking her hand.

Then Linda sat forward suddenly and grabbed at her head, "Oh my God it hurts!" she said. She was thrown back by this unseen force. Again we soothed her. We could feel the entity being dragged up her body and off the top of her head, yet the demon fought the banishment every inch of the way. Finally, it was over.

Linda collapsed back on the bed, sobbing as her breathing slowly recovered. In a few minutes things returned to normal. "Has it gone? Has it really gone?" Linda asked.

"Yes, it's gone Linda. It's over," I said. I noticed the red marks were still visible around her neck.

When she recovered, we checked her, scanning and giving some healing to fill the spaces where this entity had resided. We were relieved to see Gemma's aura was unaffected by the actions of this disembodied spirit. We then began the process of checking the remainder of the house.

As soon as we entered Gemma's bedroom I could feel a darkness that made it so I wanted to stand with my back against the wall to stop whatever was watching us. The room was cold, dark, and dismal, and the pale lilac colors did nothing to lift the vibration. To make it worse, the light bulb had blown out, and we were reliant on the light from the hallway. This only added to the sinister atmosphere. Then low, scratching noises emitted from the wardrobe.

"Did you hear that?" Bill asked.

Lyn smiled and nodded as she pointed towards the bottom of the wardrobe.

Then came another sound from the other side of the room.

"It's here isn't it?" Bill said while holding his arm out, and then reaching down to the ground. I nodded, and so did Lyn and Paul.

There in Gemma's room we found two lost souls in need of rescue. One was cowering in the corner and the other hiding in the wardrobe. First we turned our attention to the spirit in the wardrobe. It needed very little assistance from us or the other side. It saw the doorway and hopped over. The one in the corner by Bill also required very little help from anyone to be sent back to the other side.

We threw a huge silver net over the whole room and pulled it, dragging any residual energy through the doorway. We then used mini tornadoes to revitalize the vibration in the room. Once we had cleansed the house and exchanged the energy, the place began to feel much better. Within moments the dull living room appeared much brighter and at last warmth began to seep through the home.

It was difficult to understand how this demon had managed to enter into our world. Gemma and Linda thought the neighbors were using a Ouija board and that was why they had found arrows in the salt pointing towards the adjoining wall. Bricks and mortar are no boundary for ghosts or demons, so as a precautionary measure I built walls of energy that extended deep down into the ground and high above the ceilings in between the two properties.

Hopefully this would seal the place off from further onslaughts.

Five

Incubus and Succubus

There are records of the existence of incubi and succubi dating back before the birth of Christ. These demons are shape-shifters who present themselves as beautiful beings, but in reality they are small, ugly, and hideous creatures.

The incubus is a male demon who stalks female humans and attempts to have sex with them in a dream state, and the succubus is a female demon who stalks male humans and, like the incubus, attempts to have dreamtime sex with the man. It is sometimes thought they are one entity that can change their gender depending on the sex of their victims. As noted, they interrelate with their victims via the dream state. The victim is lulled into thinking what is being experienced is an erotic dream with a beautiful being. In reality, the victim's energy is drained from them through the chakras or power points of their bodies during the dream experience. These demons are not really seeking sexual gratification but rather are in search of our chi or life force, and this makes them the true psychic vampires.

Anyone who has been subjected to an attack by either of these demons will speak of being incredibly drained to the point of being physically ill. It is believed that over a sustained period of time, these attacks can have a serious impact on the general health of the victim.

These demons are fearless and incredibly powerful and their successful expulsion requires the psychic strength of several experienced mediums working with the other side. Incubi and succubi are intelligent and cunning, and they often trap lost souls in their vibrations as a means of increasing their power. These lost souls are used by the incubus and succubus to help them avoid detection. They are a force to be reckoned with. They will try to plant slivers of energy in the auras of mediums—or anyone they come into contact with—as a means of free passage back to this dimension.

Here are some of the cases we have dealt with involving these demons.

The Incubus Victim

In this case, there seemed to be a bit of divine intervention at work.

Halloween was fast approaching when Donna went to an appointment with her hairstylist Brenda. During the course of their time together, and probably because of the upcoming holiday, the conversation turned to the subject of hauntings. For the next twenty minutes or so, the discussion ranged across many different subject areas relating to the etheric world—and this included ghosts and ghouls. Brenda just happened to be a regular attendee of a local spiritualist church.

Donna had told no one outside of her family of the difficulties her daughter Vicky was facing. Neither of them had any idea who to turn to for help and the sexual nature of their problem proved to be a further barrier. Now, as her hairdresser spoke, Donna began to see a glimmer of hope. Coincidentally, the conversation between Donna and Brenda occurred just at the point when Vicky's problem had resurfaced.

With great courage, Donna decided to tell Brenda the whole story of what had been happening to her daughter. The tale spanned a period of eight years during which time her innocent child had been subjected to regular episodes of what could only be described as rape by a ghost.

Brenda listened as Donna described the events in detail. When Donna was done talking Brenda sprang into action. She reassured Donna that while she had never heard of anything like this, she knew a person who did. With Donna by her side Brenda contacted the president of her local spiritualist church and explained the situation. The president then contacted me.

I learned that Vicky was in her mid-twenties and since the age of sixteen she had been haunted by a male entity. The attacks began when Vicky lived at home with her mother and re-commenced after she had moved out and was living with her partner. Against her will, and on a regular basis, this entity had forced himself on her and she believed that he was having sexual intercourse with her. There was no time to waste.

I knew this call would require the presence of another female in addition to myself, but when I called Karen, she wasn't available. I finally got in touch with Linda and she agreed to be present. I also wanted Martin there for his healing ability. With a hastily formed team of Paul, Bill, Martin, Linda, and I, we assembled outside Vicky's tiny apartment on a cold December night. We stood in the freezing, driving rain and confirmed our respective roles, harmonizing our energies in preparation for the work ahead. I felt driven to insist that Martin was the healer and this was to be his role. Further, Paul was to anchor and manipulate the energy. Bill, Linda, and I would be the seeing and hearing forces, and I was to lead the event. It was only afterwards that I realized I had not been driven at all—it had been the other side calling the shots.

We proceeded to seal off the apartment and then made our way to the front door.

Donna came downstairs to let us in and seemed surprised by how many of us were there. I was grateful for the team that had assembled, as every bone in my body was telling me this was going to be an extremely tricky, and probably rough, time. We needed all the power we could get, and this was explained to Donna. If we failed, Vicky's life would become more unbearable—if that was possible—and believe me, it was possible.

As we all trooped up the stairs, Donna asked us to take off our shoes on the landing before we went into the small, one-bedroom apartment. We all did as requested.

As soon as we entered we could feel that the atmosphere was charged. The request for us to remove our shoes was no innocent thing—I knew it was a ploy by the entity to exploit one of my weaknesses.

Before I got a chance to say anything further, Bill said quite abruptly, "This entity is playing games here; we need to get on with it!"

I knew, though, that I couldn't begin to work until I had solved the shoe issue—because all I could think of now was my bare feet. I explained to Vicky that I couldn't work without my shoes on. This entity was working to distract me.

Without further ado, Donna fetched my shoes. While Vicky did not allow anyone wearing shoes to go into the apartment, on this occasion she made an exception to the rule, and now I could begin to work.

We chatted for a few minutes and Vicky explained that this entity was indeed raping her on a regular basis. She didn't hesitate or mince her words; she came right out with it. This was not surprising as she had lived with this for so many years. There was no need for niceties or pretense any more.

Vicky went on to explain how it all began.

At the age of sixteen, Vicky had been walking home one night from a friend's house. Halfway home she became aware of a man following her. She managed to catch a glimpse of him when he came to a stop by a hedge. He was dressed in dark blue and was around 5'8" tall with dark hair and he was very unkempt. He never moved but simply stood staring at her. She set off quickly for home and she could feel him following her. When she began to run, so did he. By the time she reached home she was hysterical and she told her mother and stepfather about the man. Furious, her stepfather ran from the house and looked up and down the street, then ran around the corner but could find no one. It was from this point that the raping commenced.

We assessed and analyzed our surroundings. While the charged atmosphere heightened our senses, it became clear that the entity was linked to Vicky and not the property. Vicky continued with her story.

Vicky explained that the situation was always the same. She would wake up in the early hours of the morning to the smell of burnt cookies. As soon as she became aware of this odor she knew what was going to happen. The smell would be followed by pressure on her chest as if there was a weight on her body and then she would physically feel the entity entering her.

Vicky said when she was eighteen her aunt—upon learning of what was happening—had told her to stand up to the entity and tell it no and it would cease its attacks. If she did this, the aunt said, Vicky would be able to overpower the thing and it would stop. So Vicky had done as her aunt instructed and to her surprise the attacks did stop—then two years later it had started all over again. This time she was unable to stop the rapes; even though she stood up to the entity once again, she found it was too strong for her. Then other sinister things began to happen. Vicky would wake up and see a man's face in the television screen, so she knew what he looked like. There also became associated with the man a strong scent of dirt and oil.

A clearer picture of this entity began to emerge. He wore dirty blue overalls and had shoulder-length dark hair. The hair was what totally freaked Vicky out as it seemed that it had grown longer since his last visitations.

I felt compelled by White Feather to direct Vicky into her bedroom. Once there I explained that we needed her to get on her bed so we could entice the entity out. We knew he was hiding behind her and we wanted him to come forward so we could deal with him. Vicky became extremely anxious and almost terrified of having to see the entity again, not to mention being subjected to his vile attack. I couldn't promise her that she wouldn't see the entity, but I could promise that he would not be able to hurt her because we would protect her. A very reluctant Vicky came into the bedroom, bringing her mother and partner with her. As we began to enter Vicky's bedroom she told us that the room was cold.

"Is the heating broken?" I asked.

"No, it's always cold," Vicky said.

The cold in the room hit us like an icy blast. Linda and I exchanged glances; we couldn't believe the difference in the temperature between the bedroom and the other parts of the apartment.

We got Vicky to take a seated position on the bed with pillows propping her up for comfort. We then placed ourselves strategically around Vicky. Apart from the dreadful cold, the room had a feeling of suppression, which made us all very uncomfortable. There was also a strong sensation of something sinister being present and this was in tandem with the sense of being watched closely.

Yet, there was also a benevolent presence in the room, and it came with the scent of lavender. Vicky noted that this was her grandmother, and she was very pleased this spirit was with her.

Everyone agreed that the corner by Vicky's side of the bed was probably the worst place in the whole room. The atmosphere in this corner was so bad that no one wanted to be there. As I stood there, I had the sensation of something like a cloak of darkness wrapping itself around me and this evoked fear from the top of my head to the tips of my toes. Martin offered to come to that part of the room, but White Feather impressed upon me that we needed a female energy in that spot. Because I was overseeing the event, it wasn't appropriate for me to stand there, so Linda moved into position in that corner.

We now began in earnest to entice the entity out and move it away from Vicky.

Suddenly Vicky burst into tears. She was clearly distressed. "I can feel something pressing down on my chest! I can't breathe!" She gulped and gasped for air. "Mom! Mom!" she called out.

With closed eyes, her hand groped for her mother. "Mom! Where are you? Help me!"

Vicky's mom looked on helplessly, not knowing what to do and totally distressed by her daughter's anguish. I asked Donna to get onto the bed and hold Vicky's hand. Donna did as I asked.

What had been a slow start now suddenly accelerated with lightning speed, and several things happened at once. Martin stepped forward to use his healing ability to reduce the effect the entity was having on Vicky. Of course we knew the sole purpose of the entity was to upset Vicky to such a degree that she wanted the clearing stopped. But to halt the operation, she had to ask us to do so.

I continued to speak to Vicky in an effort to calm her down, but she continued to gasp for breath. We could all see the distress this was creating for Donna and for Vicky's boyfriend, but, to their credit, they both remained calm and offered words of comfort to Vicky. At the same time Martin healed Vicky, the other side began peeling the beast off her and severing its ties to Vicky. We put forth all our earthly energy and blasted away at this thing while the other side worked with us. As the beast loosened its grip, it began looking for somewhere to go and, indeed, we knew it would be easier to knock this beast off one of us rather than Vicky—so my choice for this was Linda.

As the demon tried to look for an escape, I tried to manipulate it towards Linda so that the final stage of the clearance could take place.

But the demon had other ideas.

This beast knew that if it could stop me it had a chance of survival, so it came *at* me! I actually felt it climb onto my back. Then it began to mold itself around my back and arms as it started to dig itself in and hide from the others. I didn't feel hands on my hands now, but I did feel claws. I quickly called out for Martin, who was already aware of what was happening. I asked Linda to take command of the event. As I spoke, I noticed my voice had changed to a much deeper tone and I now realized that the entity had a very powerful hold over me. White Feather urged me to be still and quiet, and I did as he requested.

The rest of the group turned their attention to me, and with the aid of White Feather and the group's guides and spirit workers they began the process of digging every ounce of this demon from my energetic field. All of the team worked steadfastly together and, after what felt like an age, they began to make progress. Eventually, they were able to open a doorway behind me and push the beast through. As it began to leave, I saw a long, scaly tail trailing away from me. The next time I spoke, my voice was back to normal.

The other side continued their work and pulled the entity through. At last it was banished from Vicky, and from our world, back to its own dimension.

The room suddenly began to feel nice and warm. While one might expect this with seven people crammed into a limited space, the change was instantaneous and most welcome. There was also a lightness that permeated the area and, before we could comment, Donna said how much lighter it felt. Linda explained this was a regular occurrence after a clearance.

From the comfort of her bed, Vicky asked if her grandmother was still here.

"Of course," I replied. Then I went on to give her a message from her grandmother, who had with her a lavender bag and flowers.

Vicky was so pleased. She explained she was afraid that we might have removed her spirit grandmother when we did the clearance. It was apparent that Vicky relied on her grandmother to help her and, in fact, she stated her grandmother had tried but had been unable to do anything to stop this demon.

As a team we replaced the energy in the room with love and light and then went into the living room. Before we left I gave Vicky a prayer of protection to say every day—a prayer that would keep her safe.

We said our goodbyes, leaving behind a much happier Donna, Vicky, and boyfriend than when we had first arrived. We could all see the difference in Vicky's face and in her aura. She was free of something that had haunted her on and off for many years.

Before we got into our cars, we chatted for a bit and found we had all had uncomfortable feelings in our solar plexus while banishing the demon. It would appear that throughout the event, it had been attacking each and every one of us as it tried to hit our energy source.

As I drove home, I couldn't help but wonder why this entity had become attached to Vicky. She had done nothing to invite it into her life and this baffled me. I eventually determined that Vicky was simply in the wrong place at the wrong time.

That night I was totally exhausted, so I went to bed on my own. As soon as I got onto the bed and turned off the light, I felt I was not alone. I decided to dismiss the notion and go to sleep. No sooner had I fallen asleep than I awoke to the sound of discordant piano notes, as if someone had hit several keys together at once. The sound lasted only a few seconds, but it was loud enough to wake me.

But the sound was separate to me. As a medium/clairvoyant, when I receive a communication, it is part of me and close to me, not separate. This sound caused every fiber of my being to contract in fear and alertness. In a split second, I knew what was happening.

Vicky's entity had been pushed through the doorway and was now residing in the astral plane. We had taken extra care to ensure the whole entity had gone through the doorway because if anything was left behind, even a tiny sliver, it would give the demon a chance to communicate with the person with whom a link had been planted. In other words, that tiny sliver it had planted in me was in preparation for me to become the next victim! I recalled that when we left the house I had a niggling feeling that my aura had not been fully cleansed of this demon and, in fact, I had mentioned it to the group. I should have insisted that they double-check my aura.

Somehow I knew this was being presented to me as a test. I could feel the demon's power, but I could also feel my own strength. I began to practice everything I had ever preached—I reinforced my protection by calling in four guides: Quan Yin, White Cloud, White Feather, and Saul. I then spiked my energy with a huge force to throw off anything that had clung to me. I never felt so centered or calm as I did that night. I told the entity that it did not belong here and evoked my right to ask for it to be removed, stating it was infringing on my rights. I then commanded all my guides to remove the entity and forbade it to communicate with me in any way, shape, or form. After about five minutes, I felt its presence leave me and I knew that last particle of energy planted by the demon was gone. I checked my aura and checked it again. Yes, I was definitely free from whatever had made that dreadful sound. I had successfully cleared my own aura of this negative energy. Had it gone unchecked, it would have, over time, leeched off me and frightened me as it grew and grew into something I would have been unable to deal with.

A few weeks later, I was quite surprised when I bumped into Vicky in one of the large department stores in Birmingham. Amidst the racks of women's clothing, we exchanged pleasantries and I asked her how she was. She assured me she was fine and that there had been no further occurrences. She had only had one incident when in her dream state something quite sinister had come and dug its claws into her face. In her dream she shouted "No!" but it seemed she may have actually shouted with her voice, frightening her partner.

Vicky was concerned that because of her own doubt this demon might return, but then she seemed to reconsider and said it would never happen again.

I couldn't help but think what a persistent thing this demon was. It was not giving up without a fight—but I also knew in my heart that this was one battle the demon was going to lose.

Just before we left, Vicky told me how, for over a week, the whole apartment smelled of lavender. "I hate it," she confessed, "but grandma used to give us bags of it to put in our dresser drawers when we were kids." She noted that the smell was often so strong that her partner and visitors to the apartment remarked of the scent—even though there was not a bit of lavender in the place.

Are You Growling at Me?

Like most people who contact me, Annie was at the end of her tether. Never having been involved with anything like this before or having known anyone who had, she didn't know what to do. Being lost as to who to call when faced with the paranormal is one thing, but there are also the things that go along with it, like self-doubt. Questions assail the victim who, like Annie, wonder if the problem is her, or even her imagination.

In any event, the paranormal activity in the home Annie had occupied for eighteen years had now reached fever pitch and Annie was beginning to fear for her daughter Sarah's safety.

Annie and Sarah lived in a modern three-bedroom end terrace house. By Annie's report, odd things had often happened but never to the extent that they were happening now. Annie's main focus was the shaking of her daughter's bed. Apparently this shaking was so violent at times that it had physically thrown Sarah out of the bed. Annie also spoke of seeing a shadow standing over her while she was in bed. The sensation of waking up and feeling something pressing down on her was incredibly frightening. Lights also glowed in the cupboard underneath the stairs.

Then there were the physical complaints. Annie said she was always tired and suffered from constant headaches. In fact, anyone who stayed at the house complained of headaches, and it was constant. I had heard enough.

As usual the team gathered outside the property. This time Paul, Lyn, Bill, and I were joined by Beverley, a proficient psychic and energy worker. We knocked on the door and entered the house together.

We began in the kitchen. We searched and scanned the home's ethereal vibration and I was able to psychically pick up some information.

I said to Annie, "This house sits on the site where an old terrace once stood." Annie confirmed this by stating they were still finding old bricks in the back garden.

I then went on to tell her there was a psychic aura and imprint of the old house sitting across the back of the present house. I immediately sensed an old man wandering around. I turned to the group and asked, "This is not the problem though, is it?"

Lyn looked at me and smiled; she raised her eyes towards the ceiling, her gaze indicating the room above. Bill and Beverley were already beginning to set off upstairs in search of the unwanted occupant.

The only people present in the house that evening other than our group were Annie and her good friend Jo, who was a competent medium. We cautioned both of them to stay with us at all times; it wasn't Jo who concerned us, it was Annie.

We went directly to the room above the kitchen, which was Sarah's room. The bedroom was fitted out with stylish built-in wardrobes that ran the length of the room. Everything matched perfectly, from the curtains to the quilt cover to the carpet in lovely shades of plum and cream. Yet, despite it all, an underlying sinister ambience prevailed here.

It took us a moment to realize this room appeared to be covered in a mist. This was not a faint mist that could barely be made out—no, this was a thick mist that hung over the whole room; it was so dense it was getting difficult to see the room clearly. It was as if a fog had descended down on this warm spring evening and it only existed in this room—it did not even extend to the landing.

The fog was not only impairing our vision, making it difficult to see the bedroom, but it also seemed to be interfering with our ability to think. None of us could pinpoint precisely what was going on as we were truly having a hard time thinking straight. We were momentarily confused and fragmented.

I suddenly realized this was a ploy meant to stop us from working. I got the group together, because fragmented we are weak and vulnerable. I shouted at them to stop what they were doing and to regroup. Realizing the ploy had failed, the mist began to fade and disappear as quickly as it had formed.

We were now focused and working as one. As we scanned the room I felt drawn to the far left corner where I could sense a fearless beast glaring back at me.

"Check out the corners!" I instructed.

In seconds Lyn shouted, "It's there!" she said, pointing to the same spot where I had sensed the entity.

We began to sculpt the energy around the being to bring it into the middle of the room.

Together we moved and boxed the entity into a very small area on top of the bed. It didn't bother to cloak itself with a human disguise but showed itself in all its evilness.

I became aware of a birdlike head and featherless wings. I stopped for a moment and asked the others to describe what they were seeing.

Bill said, "This is not very tall. About three feet I would say."

"I sense a birdlike head," Beverley said.

"I know it sounds strange," Lyn said. "I feel wings, but there are no feathers on them."

Beverley chimed back, "This creature is not of this world, and it is very angry."

I felt my stomach contract, because I knew immediately what this was—it was not some lost soul—this thing was a demon. We were dealing with an incubus!

There was no way I could sugarcoat what I was about to say. I turned to Annie and very directly said, "Annie, have you had the sensation that something is having intercourse with you?"

The question astounded her, and I could feel she was bewildered. There was nothing else spoken about the subject. I placed a comforting hand on her arm and gently patted it. I was afraid to think what the thing had done to her daughter. But at least now we knew what we were dealing with and we could act accordingly.

These demons are afraid of no one and are notorious for moving from victim to victim, and I knew it would attempt to latch onto any one of us when we tried to banish it.

As we began the process of trying to knock the entity out of this dimension we shielded Annie, and Jo threw in her power to help us—but suddenly Beverley stopped and shouted, "I can feel something on me!"

Here we go, I thought.

With her eyes shut, Beverley focused on her own aura as she tried to detect where this demon lay. We were already onto it, having faced this scenario numerous times before. We were not going to be fooled again.

As usual, our guides and their helpers worked with us. Together we swiftly removed all traces of the demon from Beverley's energetic field. Now that we had it held in a small, confined space we began the final steps to remove it from this world. We could hear it screech as it tried to battle with us. Every time it tried to jump, we moved and flexed the surrounding energy to hold it captive. At the same time, the powers of the other side moved in and sucked the demon through the open portal that had been created.

Immediately afterward, we scanned and checked everyone in the room for implants, shards, or fragments of this demon's vibration. We worked as one, moving from person to person, scanning and cleansing. Each time we discovered shadows of the entity's energy, we removed it and replaced it with high vibrational energy.

After all traces of the demon's energy had been removed from us we began to scan and check the room to find out if the demon had held any other spirits captive. Almost immediately we found a very angry man who caught us all off guard by jumping into Lyn's energy without her permission. Lyn stood perfectly still, determined not to trap it in her own vibration. No words needed to be spoken, because I had noted the change in Lyn.

"Lyn, something has just joined you," I said.

Lyn nodded, smiled, and moved her stance in order to adjust her vibration. Then, with her usual restraint, she placed her hands behind her back and held her own wrists. This was her only safety mechanism; she knew from experience that when an angry spirit co-joined, there was a strong possibility she would strike out.

A dark shadow began to cover the lower half of Lyn's face, giving the impression of a man with a five o' clock shadow. Her face also appeared to be longer and her hair shorter. We could all now clearly see a male figure overlaying her whole body.

Before anyone could speak, Annie suddenly pointed at Lyn and said, "I can see my ex-partner! That's my ex-partner!"

As Annie spoke, her gaze darted from Lyn to her friend Jo as she registered total disbelief. Annie was searching Jo's face for verification. Annie wondered if Jo could see what she was seeing—and, of course, Jo could. Jo affirmed this with a nod. I think we were all taken aback that Annie was able to recognize her deceased ex-partner, who would have been Sarah's stepfather, superimposed on Lyn's body. We were used to seeing this type of occurrence, but Annie was no psychic—yet such was the strength that her ex-partner came through with.

Annie turned to Jo again, "Do you see him?" she asked frantically.

"Yes," replied Jo, "I can."

Then Lyn raised her head and met my gaze; I could feel the anger of this man pouring out of her.

I asked Lyn, "Is this who has been shaking the bed?"

Lyn nodded in the affirmative.

Something didn't seem right to me. Why would this man be trying to terrify his stepdaughter? Truly, the power this entity had generated in order to show himself to Annie was immense. In reality I would expect him to be trying to hide from his ex if he was the one frightening Sarah.

And then things became a lot clearer.

Between Lyn and me we were able to convey to Annie that her ex-partner was not trying to frighten Sarah; he had been trying to protect her. It would seem the incubus had turned his attention from Annie to Sarah, and Annie's ex had used every inch of his power to violently shake Sarah's bed. By doing this, he had been able to wake up his stepdaughter and stop the incubus from violating her. This was the message he wished to convey to Annie. Content that Annie now understood his intentions, his anger dissipated and he became peaceful. Without any further prompting he left Lyn's aura, stepped back, and walked directly into the light that awaited him.

We were convinced our work was complete. We had done what we needed to do and had cleared the upstairs. We knew there were still things downstairs to deal with, but we had removed the main entity—or so we thought.

With urgency in his voice, Bill said, "Sandrea, we must go to the next bedroom! There is something left in there and it is hiding up in the corner!"

We followed Bill's lead and began to check the bedroom he had indicated. We scanned the room and, almost immediately, all of us detected a little girl with blonde hair set in perfect ringlets. She was wearing a beautiful, layered floral dress and was standing with her back to us. We all relaxed a bit as the only thing here seemed to be this young girl.

Suddenly I became aware this was not as it appeared to be. It was something quite sinister masquerading as a being it definitely wasn't. We had another demon here— a demon of deception—and with our barriers down we were now vulnerable.

Slowly, the little girl turned her head towards us. With urgency, White Feather impressed upon me that I should not look at her face, and he instructed me to tell the others the same thing, and quickly, which I immediately did.

By combining all of our energies, we were able to trap the entity, create a doorway, and within moments the thing flew through the open portal, which we sealed. The thing was now gone forever.

We checked and scanned the remainder of the upstairs, but there was no sign of the fog and the area felt much lighter and brighter. In fact, Annie noted that the area felt lighter now in the fading daylight than it did during daytime.

We moved downstairs to deal with the cupboard under the stairs. There we found the spirits of two children and a dog that had been hiding from the darkness that had prevailed upstairs. A sheath of light had been placed over the existing doorway as a means of keeping the children safe. It was as if they knew they were now safe and the evil that had pervaded upstairs was gone. We removed the wall of light and these two children, who were dressed in Victorian clothing, skipped with their dog beside them to the other side.

We then became aware of a ley line running through the middle of the house. Somewhere along this line the demons who had resided here had found a weakness or gap in the veil, and this had allowed them entrance into our world. How and why this had happened we were not quite sure, although we thought maybe there had been some earthquake activity because this would have caused a rip in the veil.

As always we scanned, checked, and replaced any leftover residual negative energy with white and silver flowing light. We sent Mexican waves wall to wall and placed spirals of energy in every corner. Like small tornadoes, Mexican waves travel around the rooms, gathering any traces of the dark energy that had built up over a period of time.

Exhausted and convinced our work was done, we began to relax a little. The only thing left to understand was Annie's ex-partner. He had been no match for the demon and he knew it. He couldn't stop its onslaught on his former partner and when it began shifting its focus from Annie to his stepdaughter he couldn't help either. So, we reasoned, he most likely took the attitude that if you cannot beat them, you join them. And for this decision he paid a terrible price.

While the incubus thought it had found a fresh victim, the ex-partner had other ideas of ways to protect Sarah, and so the bed shaking began. Unfortunately for him it was too late. He had come from the other side, from the light. He was not a trapped spirit, but he had sacrificed his own freedom in order to protect Annie and her daughter. The demon had imprisoned him and was using him for its own good. Annie's ex-partner was now held captive in the vibration of the incubus. He gave up his right to freedom and to return to the world of spirit in order to save his stepdaughter. He would, we knew, remain captive, held by the demon, until such time as someone was able to rescue him. The sacrifice he had made had been great in order to protect Sarah.

A Succubus

For some reason, attacks on females by an incubus appear to be more frequent than succubus attacks on males.

On the other hand, it may be that females find it easier to discuss sexually related onslaughts more than men—but there is always the exception to the rule.

John was a truly gifted medium who had worked for years developing his skill, and because of his talents as a medium I eventually came into contact with him.

John had moved into a house that had a succubus already in residence, thus making him a true victim of circumstance, for he certainly had done nothing that would have attracted such a demon otherwise. He had sought and received help with his problem from various people, such as other mediums, healers, and experts, but no one appeared to be able to rid him of this entity. Indeed, after each visit from outside help, the onslaughts became worse, almost as if the demon became angered by the audacity of John trying to move it on.

This demon was in this house with its captives. Sometimes captives are made to do things to help harvest the psychic energy. Other times, and in most cases, they are low vibration themselves and enjoy the power they wield over their victims through fear. These demons or demonic forces will look for wandering or lost souls and hold them in their energy fields. The demon now has several sources harvesting the dark vibrations they crave, as more energy makes them stronger.

There were various types of attacks John had undergone from this demon and its captives. He had been subjected to physical attacks where crockery had been thrown at his head. He had awoken in the morning to find his body covered in scratches and bite marks. On several occasions, an unseen force had tried to push him down the stairs. Lightbulbs often exploded when he walked into a room. Then John became convinced that the entity had done something to the wiring in the shower and the whole unit had become live and almost killed him! All of these horrible occurrences were on top of the sexual attacks.

John approached me following a workshop I was running and asked if it was possible that he was being psychically attacked. As he spoke, I felt his guide move closer to me and watched as the guide nodded his head in affirmation. I told John I would talk to the team, which I did, and we decided to do all we could to help. Martin, Paul, and Karen joined me on this case.

At John's apartment we encountered no dark, foreboding, or sinister vibrations, because he had cleansed the energy on a regular basis. In some ways this made it more difficult for us to work because we were without the usual prompters—pockets of dark vibrations, cold spots, and spaces where we might feel very uncomfortable—all the indicators of a dark force being present.

Thanks to John's guide, I became aware of an entity that was hiding in an adjacent property. It had taken to moving between the two properties whenever another expert visited. In fact, in a dream I'd had the night before, a very solemn-looking ancient being advised me to look beyond John's apartment to find the perpetrator. Prior knowledge such as this was usually a sign that we were to have a battle on our hands. This would certainly prove to be true in this case.

During the course of the clearance we found not one but two other entities at this site. John believed one of these lost souls had actually committed suicide in the apartment and in the act of doing so had somehow become trapped. The other was a lost soul who had become entangled in the demon's vibration. We would later learn the names of these spirits were Matthew and Simon, with Simon being the one who had committed suicide.

While the succubus moved and darted away from us, this diversionary action was not of fear on its part, because this demon feared no one. The driving force was a desire to stay where it was, because it was happy with this location. It had control over two other souls and an endless supply of energy.

This succubus knew what we were capable of, and it had no intention of going anywhere; now it was in war mode. In an effort to remain undetected, it threw Matthew and Simon at us as diversion. We did choose for the time being to ignore the demon and focused our attention on Matthew and Simon. Because we had sealed the property with the help of our guides when we arrived, we were confident the seal could not be broken, even by the succubus. Once a property is sealed in light, the energy imprisons the demonic force.

We worked together to move the two lost souls from the apartment back to where they belonged. Matthew needed very little prompting from us. When the doorway opened to the other side he became aware of the gentle energy of his mother beckoning for him to walk towards the light. He turned his focus away from the apartment and purposefully moved towards the loving arms of his mother without once looking back.

Simon, on the other hand, was a totally different being. He had relished the darkness and had basked in the fear and misery he had created. Now he was trapped and he was alone and afraid. Matthew was gone and he had been abandoned by the succubus. He didn't want to walk towards the light, because he was afraid of the repercussions he would reap for his evil deeds—deeds not done during his life but done since he had passed over. Simon was not going through the doorway on his own accord. He darted around the room, smashing himself against the walls as he tried to find a weakness in the vibrational fence that held him, and, of course, there was none.

Finding no other way out, Simon turned his attention to us in the group, looking for the weakest member—or any weakness—that he could use to continue his evil existence.

We were having none of it and neither were our guides and their helpers. With a far bigger battle to come, we could not afford to waste energy on this entity. With the walls of light drawn in Simon was truly boxed. The etheric world began its work and within a few minutes the entity was removed from this plane and returned to where it came from. Once he had crossed over, we knew Simon would be healed and rehabilitated. We now moved our focus to the succubus.

The beast hid and dodged from us, but eventually we were able to trap it in the living room. With nowhere else to go it climbed onto John's back, shrank itself down, and tried to hide. This entity went from the size of a small child to miniscule in order to avoid detection.

In situations like this our greatest asset is our team's healer, and this demon was no match for Martin. In a very short period of time Martin found the entity nestled below John's shoulders. Now the succubus was well and truly trapped. Our guides drew forward as they began the process of removing the succubus. Realizing its dilemma, the entity slowly and intently rose from its hiding place, came around the side of Paul, and reached out towards me. She outstretched her claw foot and plunged deep inside my solar plexus.

Karen saw what was happening and shouted, "Sandrea, it's trying to climb to you!"

"It's too late," I said, "It's already here!"

I felt the penetration immediately. It was like being hit with a bolt of fear as the demon's claw pushed deep into my chakra. Panic began to rise up within me and it took every ounce of strength I had to maintain my composure and refuse to accept this feeling of fear as my own. I was now out of the game and totally reliant on my team to take control of the situation to remove this entity from me. I had to hold my vibration in total stillness and complete calm—otherwise I would trap the vibration of the succubus in mine. I could neither speak nor move.

Almost immediately Karen, Martin, and Paul were thrown into utter confusion because none of us had been expecting this. We had never dealt with this predicament before. When they saw my fear they sprang into action. I knew the team would never let anything harm me and that they would fight till the end. Trusting in this knowledge, I stood back and prayed they could handle it without me.

Karen took charge and began to control the whole operation. Paul provided the power and Martin used the full force of his healing ability to knock the demon off me. With the aid of their guides and mine, the team began the task of shifting the entity back to where it belonged. To me, those few minutes felt like a lifetime. Seconds before Karen said the demon had gone, I felt it leave. It was as if a giant reptile had flown off my back. In the aftermath, I could still almost smell the demon's rancid breath on the back of my neck and my solar plexus still hurt from the presence of the entity's claw. I could also feel a gaping ethereal hole where the succubus had tried to nestle. Martin soon set about filling the space with light, thus healing my aura. As wave after wave of fear swept through my body, it took every ounce of my strength to hold my essence in a vibration of love.

It was over at last and John was now free of his tormentors who had gone, never to return.

Another Incubus

I am adding this tale of an incubus here because of its relevance to the chapter. It further points out the power of this particular demon.

In my first book, *Spheres of an Unseen World*, I mentioned the idea of the incubus. I told the story of Marie and her daughter and how Marie had woken in the middle of the night to feel a heavy weight lying on top of her. This was not the first time this had happened to her. As soon as she had felt the weight, she knew what was about to follow. On this occasion, she tapped into inner strength she didn't know she had and shouted, "No!" at the unseen demon. The strength of her refusal had stopped the incubus from seeking its gratification.

Terrified by the encounter, Marie found herself sitting bolt upright in bed. Silently sobbing, she held as close to her as she could. She could not take it in. What had just happened to her? In a daze, she stayed in the upright position with her knees tucked under her chin and reflected on the occurrence. To her surprise, and out of nowhere, a hand appeared. All she could see was the hand and the forearm reaching out of the ether to her, as if offering her assistance. Marie said that at the time she knew this hand was not good and yet, as if mesmerized, she reached out to it. The next minute she found herself hanging upside down, suspended close to the ceiling by some unseen force. The incident only lasted a few seconds, and then she somehow found herself lying on the floor in between the bedside cabinet and the wardrobe. She was physically unhurt but dazed and shocked by the experience.

On its own, this event was not enough to prompt Marie to seek help for herself. It was only after her daughter mentioned having an "odd dream" that Marie felt compelled to try to sort out the problem. The daughter had never said what the content of the dream was, but it was enough for Marie to seek help.

On the night of the clearance at Marie's house it took five of us to banish the incubus from this world. We had to ask Marie to get on the bed and entice the entity into the room. Within minutes the demon joined its energy with Marie's, and we watched as her face twitched and contorted with rage when we asked the entity to leave. Each and every one of us in that room felt an onslaught of energy as the incubus sent fear through our hearts as a form of distraction.

Eventually we managed to remove the demon and sent it packing. For years, Marie experienced nothing further. Then one night about three years later she woke to the familiar feeling of pressure on top of her. In an instant, she sat up in bed and threatened the incubus, "Don't you dare come near me ever again! No! Go!" she bellowed at it.

Her strength that night was enough to remove it, and it has never returned.

Six

Psychic Children

When paranormal activity happens around children, many people are reluctant to talk to the children about it. It is felt the subject is better left alone and to not mention it in front of the child, but the difficulty with that way of thinking is that many children are far more psychic than we take them for. Children can see and sense the paranormal activity and are often left bewildered and confused because the adults around them refuse to listen or fail to explain what is happening.

There are many, many examples of children and psychic phenomena experiences, such as children seeing the spirits of dead relatives and communicating with them quite easily. It is believed that all children are born psychic, and it is only as they become more and more entrenched in this world that they lose the ability to be able to see the spirit realm or remember all the wonderful colors associated with the etheric world.

I have always insisted that small children be removed from the property when we go to clear unwanted guests. My fear is that children are vulnerable, and it is difficult to protect them—but there have been several occasions when the activity has been around a young child, and we have had no choice but to have that child present in order to successfully clear the problem.

On each occasion we have been mesmerized by the child's ability and what the child is able to see.

Guided by the Child

Emily and her family were at a breaking point when they found me through a friend of my colleague Patrick. Patrick's friend ran a Mind, Body, and Spirit shop in Wolverhampton. For three months, Emily and her family had been re-tormented by an unseen force that was affecting the whole family, which included five children.

The torment of this family had actually begun over two decades ago. Fires would mysteriously start with no known cause, and a child had actually been pushed from an upstairs window. Disturbances had reached such a point in their previous home that they had found another property and fled from the first home in the night, bringing with them only one piece of furniture—a set of bunk beds.

They had been in their new residence for about a year with no problems and had begun to relax; they felt they were finally free from the torment that had plagued their lives for such a long period of time.

Then one day they brought the bunk beds that had been stored in the garage into the new home and all hell broke loose. Not one member of the family escaped the constant barrage of disturbances this unseen force hurled at them. The entity had been in touch with their daughter Kelly for as long as they could remember and, a short while after moving into the new house, Kelly had informed her family that Rebecca—the name Kelly used when referring to the demon—was very angry and she had been looking for them since they had moved. When Rebecca found the family, she would show them how angry she really was.

At first the family was frightened by this warning, but over time it was forgotten.

That was until the day the bunk beds came into the house. From this point on, the family seemed to be facing daily onslaughts and problems. The dogs howled without any provocation—something they had not done since they left the previous home—and no one appeared to be able to comfort them. This howling would go on for several hours. Then suddenly a very healthy two-year-old dog died without cause. Next three baby rabbits died one after the other following a threat from this demon.

Other disturbances included furniture being dragged across the floors to block bedroom doors and cuddly toys flying off the shelves. All the doors in the wardrobe units would fly open and the contents would be scattered around the room—a few minutes later order was restored when everything was returned to its rightful place by some unseen hands. In the master bedroom, the bedding would be stripped from the bed and neatly folded on top of the mattress. On each occasion, pictures of Archangel Michael and Metatron, given as a means of protecting the family, would be positioned in front of the bedding as if mocking the notion of safety.

Soon the neighbors began to complain of hearing the sound of heavy furniture being dragged around bare floorboards. This activity would last for hours and happened when the family was out. Furniture was also heard being dragged across the attic floor. A heavy ladder used to access the attic began to move on its own.

Emily and eighteen-year-old daughter Becky were further tormented by being awakened in the middle of the night to the feeling that something extremely heavy was lying on top of them. Such was the weight that they were unable to move. Both claimed they felt the weight on them was forcing the air out of their lungs, making it difficult to breathe. This had happened not just once but on several occasions.

Desperate and at her wit's end, Emily had first contacted a local paranormal group. The group had visited on several occasions but failed to provide any solutions to the family's dilemma. Their equipment did record temperature variations of 18 degrees Celsius in the hallway, but any attempts to videotape activity were flawed by the continual draining of the batteries in the recorder. Unable to get any information or gain any real evidence, the group abandoned the family.

When Paul, Lyn, Bill, Patrick, and I arrived at the property we were taken into the living room and surprised to see several people sitting and waiting for us. Present were Emily and Dave, their children Nathan and Becky, the neighbor Sarah, and Uncle John. When Patrick had arranged the gathering, he had explained that the other children should be removed from the home, so the youngsters had gone to stay with their grandfather. Emily was the one who had structured her audience, because she was desperate for someone to believe her. These people could vouch for Emily's stories as they had all had their own experiences of the terrible ghostly phenomena in this home and the previous place Emily and Dave had lived in.

After talking with those assembled for a short while, we decided it was time to prepare to get to work. Patrick would stay downstairs with Nathan, Dave, and Uncle John. The rest of us would keep Emily, Becky, and Sarah with us, as we felt these were the vulnerable people in the house and therefore needed protection.

As we climbed the stairs, I felt an unseen force pushing against me, trying to bar my way upward. It took extreme effort to be able to get past whatever was trying to block me. And I wasn't the only one feeling this force; the others remarked they were meeting this extreme resistance. It was as if there was an invisible wall across the stairs trying to stop our ascent. The force had also effectively cloaked the area in darkness and there was a feeling of impenetrable evil; it was as if this stairway were a gateway to hell.

The demon Rebecca had opened the gateway and a series of equally evil presences had been drawn into the home.

Once we got upstairs, we decided to start in Kelly's bedroom because we felt this was a key location. The room was dark, cold, and oppressive—not at all like a typical little girl's room. No matter how many lights were switched on, the artificial light appeared unable to pierce the dark atmosphere. A fetid smell also cloaked the very essence of the room.

We were determined to flush this entity out. We needed to get this thing out in the open so we could see what we were dealing with.

We began to use beams and walls of light and moved and manipulated these until we located the entity that was the cause of this dreadful atmosphere. Eventually we did get the entity trapped in a circle of light on the bed and very soon a clear image of it began to emerge. Here, before us, was a little girl with blonde curly hair in a nice Victorian dress. She appeared to be very cute and very sweet, yet no matter what angle we looked at her from, we were unable to see her face. Similar experiences in the past had taught us that what we were being shown was not what the entity truly was. Powerful demons can shape-shift and easily project an image totally unlike what they really are.

The little girl moved constantly to make sure we could not detect her true nature. We strongly suspected she was the demon with whom Kelly had conversed. We thought we had her trapped in the light, with the only way out being via the doorway we had mentally created—or so we thought. In an instant she was gone, with no help or assistance from us. She had jumped into the light, but I would later find out that she was traversing it for her own use.

With nothing left to fight, we moved on. The next room we tackled was the parents' bedroom. The three women, Emily, Becky, and Sarah were between Paul, Lyn, Bill, and me. I had positioned myself close to the door and adjacent to a heavy bookshelf.

No sooner had I positioned myself than everything began to happen at once.

As I stood I watched a shadow man walk across the wall towards me. This was followed by two others; all three could clearly be seen traversing the wall. Their long limbs were proportionally out of synch with their thin, sleek bodies. They held no other form than demons creeping about in their eerie shadow forms. Slowly and deliberately they made their way towards me.

Almost simultaneously and before I had a chance to tell the others what was happening, Emily said in a raised voice, "There is something alongside you! I can see it! Three times it has walked past! It is like a shadow, and I have seen a shadow moving on the wall there."

I could hear the panic in her voice.

As Emily spoke, she pointed directly to the spot where I had seen the shadow men walking across the wall. For me this was confirmation, because Emily had seen precisely the same shadows I had. I nodded in agreement and tried to offer words of comfort to keep her calm. I certainly didn't tell her there were three of these shadow men, preferring to let her believe there was just one.

I could see that Becky was feeling the fear as well, although Sarah remained calm, cool, and collected.

Suddenly one of the shadow men passed behind me. Before I could move, I felt a familiar tingling sensation and an inner cold began to entwine itself around me as the entity merged with me. It slid down my back and stretched its arms along mine, fitting like a glove to render me totally useless and unable to maintain control.

Emily, who had seen what was happening, shouted out, "It's there again! Oh my God, I can see it! It's there—it's in between Sandrea and the door."

I breathed a sigh of relief for Emily's outburst because now my colleagues knew precisely what had happened to me. I stood perfectly still.

The team needed no further prompting or information as they jumped into action.

Removed from the event, I stayed put while they began the process of pulling the demon off me. Suddenly Becky began to cry and called out about a "something" being in the room. Then Emily joined in saying she agreed with Becky and that she could feel the something also and she pointed to her side. This was an attack from all sides, and I was helpless.

Bill and Lyn worked together. With his usual composed and professional manner, Paul looked after the others and kept them calm and out of the way. For my safety, Paul knew he had to maintain a peaceful demeanor until the others had peeled this intruder off me. I knew the Rebecca demon was controlling this relentless onslaught from some safe zone. I could feel her glee as the attack continued. She had the keys to the gateway to hell and the occupants were hers for the choosing—and we were the victims.

The other side jumped into action and began to lead and guide Lyn and Bill. The guides increased Lyn and Bill's power to ensure they could knock this fiend off my back. During this whole time, I had not moved an inch and had started to hold a love vibration in my aura—I knew thoughts of love would make the being very uncomfortable. Sure enough, with combined effort of help from the other side, the others quickly and deftly pushed the shadow man off me through the doorway to the other side and the door slammed shut. I was aware of a fragment of energy between my shoulder blades and I knew the team would deal with this later when we met at a local bar. We would always go to a bar after each clearance to reflect on what had happened. We would also scan each other, one at a time, and then remove any blockages or slivers of energy.

For now, we began to scour the room to see what else was present. Emily and Becky were crying as they spoke of seeing several shadows through the crack in the door. They noted that the shadows appeared to be moving backward and forward as if trying to find a way in. We stopped and regrouped and again calmed Emily and Becky down. If we truly wanted to beat these demons, we needed Emily and Becky to be strong and focused. I spoke to them firmly about what would be required of them and they looked at one another, then agreed they would do their best.

Suddenly, not once, but several times, a loud, deliberate knock could be heard coming from the inside of the wardrobe. Emily reacted immediately and asked Sarah if she could hear the knock. Sarah affirmed that she could.

"We can all hear it," Bill said. "Just ignore it. The entity is trying to frighten you."

Still more bangs came as Rebecca attempted to generate more fear and confusion, because to the underworld fear means power. Whatever was in the wardrobe was a shape-shifter that thought we would be fooled into thinking it was a lost soul. We started the process of instigating its exile.

Calmly, Sarah described a sensation of tingling from head to toe. It was clear the demonic force had jumped into her energy field. Rather than acknowledge it and have it become aware that we knew where it was, I said nothing, because by ignoring it we were giving it a false sense of security and would deal with it as soon as we could.

The landing and stairs appeared to be the other center of activity. As we stood looking at the external wall, we could see it was a hive of activity. Shadows danced across the surface and strange lights flashed on and off. In fact, it almost appeared like a giant plasma screen because of the extent of activity that was taking place. We capped the space so nothing more could come through the portal.

We went to check out the room above the garage and found it was fresh and clear. The only apparent activity in this room was a large chest of drawers that was dragged across the doorway, almost as if something had tried to keep the dark forces out.

The bathroom was too small for us to all fit into. As Lyn checked it out Bill stood in the hallway, taking a well-earned break. He stood with his arms raised and pressed against the wall, using it to support his weight.

As I walked out of the bathroom I saw what I could only describe as a hag nestling in the crook of Bill's arm, between him and the wall. This creature had long, black straggly hair that covered her distorted gray face. Her grin exposed long, rotting teeth. Below her hips, her body seemed to have just faded away. She was commanding me to look at her and feel all that she could throw at me. I went to Lyn and whispered in her ear that we had a problem with Bill.

Lyn and I then asked Bill into the bathroom.

"There is something here?" he asked as he pointed to the precise area where the hag lay.

"Dead right," Lyn responded with a smile.

Bill then went on to describe the entity.

Lyn requested that Bill be silent and stand still so we could deal with the demon.

This was no hag—it was Rebecca at her worst—this was Jezabeth.

This demon had dodged us and hidden from us all night. She had thrown her henchmen into the cauldron as bait because they were disposable. When she had portrayed herself as a little girl in the bedroom, there had been motive to her actions; she knew she had to leave before the other side was ready. She knew if she acted quickly, she would be able to avoid detection.

This demon was a master of darkness and again we thought we had her trapped. She made her presence known to Lyn and then she was gone again!

We moved into the small bedroom at the front of the house to remove another entity. Here we found a lost soul— a soldier in a gray uniform was cowering in the corner by the window. Somehow he had become caught in Rebecca/ Jezabeth's trap. Now we were here to free him from his tormentor. We opened the doorway for him and watched as he furtively looked around to see if it was safe. At the same time we held a protective mental shield around him. Realizing it was okay, he rose from the crouched position and, without any guidance or assistance, he jumped into the light and was gone.

Rebecca had indeed kept her promise. She had found the family and returned with a vengeance. As Jezabeth— her true name—she was a demon and had all the powers associated with such an entity. She had the power to call other demonic forces and that is precisely what she had done. She had opened a gateway to the bowels of hell and had allowed numerous equally malevolent entities to enter into this world so they could wreak their own havoc on humanity.

We now turned our attention to Sarah and began the process of removing the entity from her aura. This was exactly the same type of being that had jumped onto my back earlier—a shadow man. We caught it off guard, and in a moment it was trapped. We could almost hear it scream as it twisted and writhed. It was going nowhere. White Feather went into action and in no time at all the entity was snatched from Sarah and dragged back to its own world.

Now we turned to Emily and Becky. We sat them both on the bed together. We could see the third shadow man had them in his grip. Again without any warning we gave this final entity no time to deploy any evasive action. It was as if this being was made of elastic as he kept a foot in each camp. His vibration was buried deep into their energy fields and he lay motionless to avoid detection. We knew he was waiting for the time when he could begin harvesting the fear from this family's energetic fields. This time the removal was a bit harder as Becky's fear created pockets for this beast to nestle into. We were also aware of Becky's tender age, so carefully and nonchalantly we eased the shadow man away from both of the women and sent it back to where it belonged.

We removed the three shadow henchmen that night and the lost soul, but we had a very strong feeling that we had not rid the family of Rebecca. She was too powerful and cunning.

We again shifted our focus to the opening on the staircase. It appeared to sit right in the middle of the steps. The majority of the activity in this area had shut down, yet we could still sense the vast portal. It was as though a shaft had opened between earth and the lower astral plane, which is sometimes referred to as hell. We offered the earthly connection and the other side did its work. The dark glow that permeated the stairs slowly began to fade as the shaft was shut down.

As we began to walk downstairs, Sarah whispered a thank you to me. We knew she had suspected that something had joined with her but had remained silent for everyone else's sake.

We now returned to the living room where Patrick had kept the remainder of those present safe.

The downstairs of the house was checked and everything appeared to be clear. At last we could relax. As we sat, a few members of the family told us some of the events that had occurred in the previous house over the past twenty-one years.

It was hard to understand how one family had been through so much and managed to survive largely unscathed. And it was not surprising they were now living with so much fear.

But we got ready to leave, hoping that we had sent every disembodied spirit and demon back to the worlds where they belonged.

We said our goodbyes to the family with promises to return if the problems resumed. We all knew when we left that we would be back to this property, although none of us would have guessed we would be back such a short while later.

I was very disturbed to receive the phone call from Emily telling me that when the small children had walked back into the house, the demon had come back in with them, and it had returned with a vengeance—this time physically attacking eighteen-year-old Becky.

According to Emily, Becky had awakened in terror, sensing that something had fallen on her bed. Terrified, she called out to her parents, and then she got up and ran to the door, but it was as if she had run into an invisible wall. She felt the full force on her face, especially her nose and eyes. Dave and Emily heard the commotion and ran to Becky's aid. When they got to Becky's room, they were met by Becky, who had a bloody nose and two swollen eyes.

Emily also said that when Kelly had come back into the house after this last visit by us she had turned to her mother and said, "Mommy, Rebecca is very angry with you. She tells me that she can no longer live with us. Is that true?"

Emily had confirmed to her daughter that what she said was correct. She told Kelly that Rebecca did not belong here and would have to go back to her own world.

"Well," Kelly said, "she says she's going nowhere yet and now we are going to pay the price."

The morning after the attack on Becky a rather glum Kelly told her parents that Rebecca was back.

That night the pictures on the wall in the living room spun frantically. This was the start of a further onslaught that would only end after the next visit by us.

It was a week before we could return to the property, and in that week the family had been subjected to a reign of terror. Becky had been thrown out of her bed once and knocked off the bed twice. Everyone in the family had been subjected to feelings of incredible fear. Their son Dan's girlfriend Emma woke up to see what appeared to be a hag with the near-typical long, black straggly hair, gray skin, dressed in black rags, running with arms outstretched towards their little girl who was sleeping soundly in her cot. It was as if the hag was about to snatch the baby and carry it away. Emma's screams of terror seemed to stop the hag from grabbing the child. The apparition then laughed hysterically at Emma, mocking her fear. This was the final act for the family, and for the remainder of the week they had slept downstairs together in the living room, because it was the only way they felt safe.

As before, the younger children were removed from the house and were spending time with the grandparents. Kelly stayed behind so I could have some time with her.

As soon as we arrived I spoke to Kelly. "Kelly, do you know why I'm here with my friends?"

This beautiful, red-headed child played with a small toy in her hand and shyly looked up and said, "Yes, you are here because we have a ghost and she is called Rebecca."

I recalled that, according to Emily, this ghost had two names, Rebecca and Jezabeth, and the name Kelly used depended on the way in which the demon showed itself to her.

"She's not a nice little girl," Kelly said as she shook her head to add effect to her words.

"Why is she not a nice little girl?" I asked.

"Because she hurts my family and she doesn't like Becky. I keep telling her Becky is a nice girl, but Rebecca doesn't think so and Rebecca wants to hurt her." As she spoke her little face looked quite sad.

"Is Rebecca here now?" I asked.

Kelly shook her head from side to side. "No, she isn't."

"Where is she?" I asked.

"She's upstairs resting, but she's coming down soon."

I asked Kelly where she first met Rebecca.

"She came to me at our old house and said she was a lonely little girl and wanted to be my friend. But she's not really a little girl and she is not nice."

I asked Kelly about the other name she called Rebecca. "It's Jezabeth. She is Rebecca until she takes her face off."

Kelly then went on in great detail and explained how Rebecca had very long fingernails and she used these to dig into her forehead and remove her face. As Kelly spoke, she raised a hand and mimicked Rebecca's actions.

Despite talking about such a harrowing subject Kelly seemed quite nonchalant and unperturbed. Then with all the wisdom of a child of nearly six years of age Kelly again stated that Rebecca was not nice. I then asked Kelly what was behind Rebecca's face when she removed it.

In a very matter-of-fact way, yet grimacing her face, Kelly said there were lots of bugs and spiders.

"Do you want to see my protection?" Kelly asked.

When I indicated that I would, she put her hand down her top and removed a little purple bag that was tied around her neck with a purple ribbon. She opened the bag and showed me some crystals and a cross. Kelly told me that Becky had a bag like this, but when she put it on it had burned her neck. This dialogue was also delivered to me in a nonchalant manner, as if Kelly were discussing any mundane topic.

It was now painfully clear that Becky was the one who had been subjected to the worst of the onslaught this time—and now Emily was worried that Becky was acting strangely, and in fact even looked a little odd. Becky also seemed unable to join in any conversation.

Emily had noticed bandages on Becky's wrists and that her daughter had developed a rash during the week, causing her to constantly scratch her arms.

This sounded like a very different Becky from the first time we had visited.

Before we could begin to focus our attention on Becky, she suddenly made a run for the door, screaming that she needed to get out of the room. She said this in a high-pitched voice. Of course we were wise to this in a split second, and Paul managed to carefully move Becky from the door. At the same time, Emily soothed her daughter and began to speak to her about us being there to help. This appeared to do the trick. It was obvious that Becky was being unduly influenced by this evil force.

Holding her by the hand, Emily gently led Becky back to the sofa, where she sat with her daughter and periodically patted her hand in reassurance.

Suddenly the atmosphere in the room became charged with fear and a dark shadow seemed to overlay the room.

Jezabeth had arrived with all her power and might. The demon had been unsuccessful in getting Becky out of the room, and now she was ready to fight the real battle.

Initially, there was no need for words between us as we watched the descent of Jezabeth into the center of the living room.

Lyn looked at me and moved her eyes towards where Jezabeth was standing. I gave a half nod in return to indicate I was seeing the demon as well. Kevin spoke of feeling a cold breeze that shot past him.

The room felt full of the dark, sinister presence that was doing its best to evoke fear from us—but we held firm against it.

Before I could speak, Kelly told us that Jezabeth was here and then she pointed to the exact spot where the demon was standing, and thus for us confirmation was complete.

I knew we had to get Becky on our side. If she didn't express her desire for Jezabeth to leave, we would not be able to proceed with the banishment. Very gently I explained to Becky that I needed her permission to remove Rebecca/Jezabeth from her. Despite her state of mind Becky immediately agreed.

This was all we needed.

We began to work. I led, and through a series of nods everyone went into action.

While we worked Kelly talked and watched us.

I had opened a doorway behind Becky in preparation to push the demon through. Kelly was able to see the mentally created doorway and spoke up about it opening behind her sister. Then Kelly noticed that something seemed to be pulling Jezabeth through the doorway, making the demon appear to be smaller and thinner.

Kelly adjusted her position to get a better look. "I can see Jezabeth being sucked through the doorway into a room. Oh dear, she doesn't want to go, but they are making her go. Now she is trying to get back through the doorway, but they won't let her. The angels are holding her in the room."

Then Kelly reported that the doorway was closing and Rebecca/Jezabeth was gone for good.

This whole interaction with Kelly was extremely interesting as at no time did any of us mention a doorway, yet the child had clearly seen it, and the entire episode, exactly as it had unfolded. Kelly was totally unbothered by the entire occurrence and, from the unflappable manner in which she spoke, one would think she was describing a rather mundane happening.

Before we had a chance to fully ascertain whether or not the demon had gone through the doorway, Kelly told all of us that the doorway was shut and Rebecca was never going to be allowed to come back again. A further bonus was that Kelly's commentary had given Becky a focus, and this had helped to keep her calm.

For the rest of our time there, Kelly continued her commentary. She went on to describe the color of the energies we had generated in the room and, again, at no time did any of the group mention the colors of the vibrations we were working with. However, Kelly was able to describe it all in great detail, especially the wonderful silver energy we had drawn in. She would see a lovely swirl of color in a particular part of the room and mention how beautiful the hues and the energies were.

Then Kelly said, "Oh look, Mommy, there are angels flying around the room. They are little angels and they are white and gold. They are making our home a happy home. Can you see them, Mommy? I can see one, two, three, four!"

Kelly watched the ceiling where the angels were flying around in a circular motion. As she watched these angels, a wonderful look of glee danced across her face and for a moment it seemed as if she were communicating with the angels.

The angels were here to look after the family and would do so for as long as they were needed.

We all noticed that the room had become warmer. The dark and dank energy had been lifted and was replaced with a lighter vibration. This change could be physically felt by all who were present.

Our work finished at last, we checked the house once more to make sure everything was clear, then said our goodbyes and left, hoping we would never have to return. In some ways this leave-taking was a sad event because we would not have the pleasure of talking to that remarkable little girl again.

As we walked towards our cars Patrick turned to me with a smile and told me that, one day, when she was older, Kelly would give me a run for my money. I laughed, because I had to agree with him.

As usual we met up at a local restaurant so we could not only get something to eat but also have time to reflect on what we had just gone through. Before we went in we took the time to check ourselves to make sure we were clear of negative energy. Once assured we had no dark vibrations clinging to our energy field we went inside.

During this time together, the conversation was mostly about the amazing gift Kelly had shown all of us.

Note: Jezabeth was a Babylonian demon who is often referred to in the feminine sense. While there is very little written about this demon, she is noted as the Demon of Falsehood and Lies. It would also appear that this demon is associated with anger and is said to follow or stay with someone for years.

A Crafty Ghost

Sarah and Kevin lived with their two small children in a semi-detached house in a local town. The house had originally belonged to Kevin's grandmother and the family had occupied it since it was built.

The problems in the house had begun about a year and a half ago when Sarah had befriended a distant cousin and allowed her to move in.

What started off with the occasional odd incident slowly began to escalate into a string of events that made everyone afraid to stay in the home. Things had come to a head about four months prior when a fire had broken out in Sarah and Kevin's bedroom. Despite a full fire investigation, the authorities were unable to determine the cause of the blaze.

Sarah became convinced a ghost was responsible.

Long after the cousin left, the problems continued to escalate. Chairs would float around the kitchen, electrical appliances turned themselves on, and the kettle would boil even when unplugged. The little boy was terrified and the baby girl would scream and cry without reason—and then red marks began to appear on her arms and face.

The list of incidents and activity was lengthy, yet on the night that Paul, Karen, Martin, and I visited, we could find nothing. We checked the place from top to bottom, inside and out, but not one disembodied spirit or demon did we find. Oh, there were pockets of negative energy as if left over from some previous event, but that was it. Several rooms were quite dark, but again we found no cause for any of the incidents described, and so less than an hour later we left, confident that if there had been anything on the property, it was no longer there. We were at a loss as to what was happening on the site. Before I left, I gave Sarah my mobile number and told her to call me in the future should any paranormal activity resume.

It didn't take long before a very distraught Sarah was in touch again—by mid-afternoon of the following day. Apparently, about two hours after we left, the problems started up again. There had been a horrific banging so loud the whole house had vibrated. The children were screaming and covering their ears to try to block the sound. So great was the level of the noise that Sarah and Kevin could not hear themselves talking. They did try to detect where the noise was actually coming from, but it appeared to be resounding from inside the walls. Also the bedroom door had slammed shut so forcefully that the wood near the hinges had splintered. While the commotion had only lasted for a few minutes, they were terrified by the incident. Then, to make matters worse, the neighbors on either side were complaining about the banging and were asking them to keep it down.

It was clear now there was a ghost or entity of some sort in the house and that it had known of our impending visit and had gone into deep hiding. Now it had returned with a vengeance.

After speaking with Sarah, I now strongly felt that I needed to speak to her son Jack. I requested that she keep him at the house until my team and I arrived.

When we got to Sarah's, Jack was sitting on her lap, cuddling her close, and sucking away on his pacifier.

"Hello, Jack," I said in a calm voice.

Still keeping the pacifier in his mouth and barely audible, Jack whispered, "Ello." He continued to cuddle up to his mom and suck on the pacifier. He was clearly very shy and made no eye contact with any of us.

At this point, I really began to wonder what I was up for. How on earth was I expected to have a conversation with a child who was barely able to talk?

I tried again. "Jack do you know any nasty men?"

From this point on, we were amazed at what this little boy managed to convey—his parents probably more so. Sarah and Kevin constantly exchanged looks with one another and total shock registered on their faces. Sarah told us that Jack didn't normally talk and Kevin nodded in agreement. It was almost as if Jack's dad was struck dumb by the ability of his little boy that night—because talk Jack did, incessantly, and what he said was incredible.

As soon as I had asked the question about the nasty man, the child purposefully removed the pacifier from his mouth and proceeded to tell me that there was a nasty man upstairs hiding in Jack's bedroom. To add effect, he pointed to his bedroom directly above the living room and told me, "Nasty man knows you can make him go away."

"Does he now?" I asked.

"Yes!" Jack said and then added, "He does not want to go away. He wants to stay here." As he spoke he nodded his head, as if affirming what he had said.

Jack needed no prompting whatsoever. He chatted and chatted, "Nasty man hid from you last time. He went to that house over there. There is a ghost in that house too." As he spoke, he pointed to a house in the distance. "When you left the man came back and he was very mad. He bangs doors." As Jack spoke, he moved his arm very quickly, imitating the action of slamming a door.

"Does your sister see him?" I asked.

Jack returned the pacifier to his mouth but quickly took it out as the child decided to show us precisely what this entity was doing to his four-month-old sister. He screwed up his face, raised his hands to his cheeks, and made clawlike fists. He then made what to him was a scary sound. "Man do this to my sister!" he said. He then went on to tell us that the man sometimes pinched his sister's arm. At this point, Sarah and Kevin nodded their heads in unison and Sarah told us that the daughter had often developed red marks on her arms that could not be accounted for.

Just before Kevin carried Jack out of the room, Jack turned to me and said, "Nasty man knows he has to go. He knows you are going to make him go home." With that, he put his arms around his father's neck, buried his face on his dad's shoulder, and wrapped his legs around his father's waist. He gave us a childlike wave as the two got ready to set off for grandpa's house, which was just around the corner.

Sarah stood shaking her head in total disbelief. She then turned to all four of us and said, "I cannot believe Jack has told you all that—that is amazing!" She turned to Kevin. "Isn't it amazing? Can you believe it?" Kevin shook his head as he agreed with his wife. Jack had certainly surprised everyone that night.

Soon afterward, we began the process of flushing out the entity. We went upstairs and, as predicted by Jack, there the ghost was, still trying to hide in Jack's bedroom. As we worked, we discovered a man in his fifties who had given his life over to drink—and he was not just a drunk. Overall this man really was a bad character, and I could imagine that his good deeds could have been counted on one hand. He had lived his life on the dark side and when passing over he had been unable to face the light, so he had chosen to stay here in this vibration. While only slightly built, his whole attitude was menacing. He was practically bouncing off the walls as he tried to find a way out of his temporary prison.

We sealed the room so that he would be going nowhere. When he realized what had happened, he tried to transmit waves of fear towards us. As I walked up the stairs, I felt a terrible sense that something so foreboding and far more powerful than me was waiting for me. This entity was trying to envelop us in a blanket of negative energy, but we were having none of it. He didn't belong here, and it was time for him to go.

Just before we began his transition, he looked at me with a sneer and said one single word, "Fire!" Then he laughed. As soon as he uttered this word the spirit world moved in with their usual speed and accuracy and returned him to the place where he belonged.

Before we left, Kevin told us something that even Sarah had not known. The house Jack had pointed to had an incident that had been reported in the local papers more than twelve years ago. At that time, the property was thought to be haunted and the family had been troubled by paranormal activity.

Seven

Haunted Places

There are a great many haunted sites in the British Isles. Here are some of the more interesting cases we have investigated.

The Meeting Place

Set in a multicultural suburb on the outskirts of Birmingham, the haberdashery and tailor shop shop had once been in the heart of a busy community and was now over a hundred years old. At the time of its creation, it would have been classified as luxurious accommodations. The large premises ranged over three floors. The ground floor was a shop and the two upper floors were the living quarters and provided a spacious three-bedroom apartment. At the rear of the property was a small yard.

The building stood at the end of some other shops. Underneath the premises were extensive cellars with two entrances. One entrance was through the rear yard and the other through large doors set into the floor of the shop. Because of its location, the cellar was designated as a bomb shelter and the general public would have accessed the shelter through the rear yard. While this access point had long gone, the cellar had not. Nowadays the only way to reach the cellar was via the large wooden door in the floor of the main shop.

The boom years after the war and the mass production of clothing saw the decline of the tailoring business, and the haberdashery store had long been gone. At the time of our visit, the shop was being used for storage and the current owners were having difficulty keeping tenants in the apartment. For whatever reason, no one appeared to stay very long. Even the staff who visited on occasion were afraid to be inside the premises on their own. They complained of hearing sounds coming from the cellar. Several other tenants had made similar remarks and there were reports of hearing someone moving around in the cellar, as well as muffled sounds and people talking to each other.

Karen, Martin, Paul, and I visited the property and it was dark when we arrived. The streets appeared to be deserted and the shop was freezing cold when we went in. There was a deep sense of neglect as dust lay on every surface. A dirty rug was pulled back to reveal two large wooden doors set into the floor. Each door had a circular handle and it took significant force to raise these huge doors into the open position. Once the doors were open, Karen and I exchanged glances with one another as we looked down into the dark hole in front of us.

The owner of the shop was present, and kindly went before us and turned on the light, which was situated at the bottom of the steps. This single bulb gave very little illumination, but it was better than nothing. Gingerly, the four of us descended down the narrow wooden steps that had a steep decline. The layers of dust were even more prominent down here in the basement than they were in the shop.

I was the first to go down the steps. As I waited for the others, I tried to brush off the dust that clung to my trousers and jacket. It seemed a hopeless thing to bother with.

The cellars were extensive. Taking in their size, it appeared they extended partly underneath the adjoining building. The whitewash that once covered the walls was dirty and peeling off. Cobwebs clung to every corner, nook, and cranny. Above our heads the bare joists in the floorboards of the shop floor could be seen. Old wooden benches rested against the walls and these were remainders of the bomb shelter. Time had definitely taken its toll on those wooden slatted benches, and many of the slats were now missing because of the damp atmosphere.

Beside the large room we were now standing in there were several smaller rooms off to the left of us. It was hard to understand their purpose, although some appeared as if they might have been food storage areas, as concrete slabs seemed to be ideal ledges. Many properties from the Victorian times were built with this type of storage. It was said that fruit, when packed in wooden boxes, could last a whole season and be as fresh as the day it was picked when it was stored in the damp atmosphere of a basement like this. Other vegetables and meats would also have been put down here and kept well.

The main room measured about 30' x 30', and according to the owner, it was suggested that up to fifty people could be housed in this area. With the low ceilings and airless atmosphere, sitting in this space must have been incredibly uncomfortable. It was thought that during the air raid drills the smaller rooms were used as makeshift toilets.

Birmingham was the third most heavily bombed city in England during World War II, and it is alleged that one raid lasted for over twelve hours. Important factories to the war effort were scattered amongst residential areas, and it was these sites that the Nazis targeted. The death toll in Birmingham from the war totaled over 2,000.

As the team moved from the main area to the three smaller rooms, we began to psychically scan each room. The smaller rooms had two more rooms off of them with less space than the previous ones. We moved from one room to the other during our search, trying to ascertain if there was anything here worthy of further investigation. Karen and

I sensed that animals had been kept in one of the smaller rooms at one time. We immediately discounted the possibility that there was any residual energy associated with their presence, and the only thing we did pick up was a mere imprint on the atmosphere.

The atmosphere was very dense, making it feel as if we were in a crowded space, yet there was only our team and the shop owner down in this large expanse.

We returned to the main room and slowly walked up and down. We noted the only piece of furniture in this area was an old cupboard resting against the exterior wall and jammed in between the benches.

I turned to Karen and said, "I feel an opening here as if there was another entrance into the space."

As I spoke, I pointed towards the cupboard and Karen nodded her head in agreement. "Sandrea, that is precisely what I was thinking. I could see a very narrow staircase and lots of people pouring down it very quickly!"

Martin and Paul had sensed the same thing.

All four of us turned towards the owner as we waited to see if he could shed any light on what we had just said. The owner quickly confirmed our findings: there had indeed been another entrance. The doorway had been bricked up in the 1960s by the former owners because the shop workers were complaining of hearing muffled sounds— as if many people were talking together in the basement. It was thought that local youths or tramps were breaking into the cellar through the external entrance, and in an effort to stop this the doorway had been bricked. It was just coincidental that the cupboard was hiding the walled-up area. If this was an entrance, there would be no bench in this space, so it made a handy slot for the storage cupboard.

We were all in agreement that the area we needed to focus our attention on was the main room, so we stood there together in silence as we tuned our psychic senses to the vibration of the space. With our guides ever present we began the process of determining if indeed there was any ghostly phenomenon in this space. What met us was amazing and no doubt will stay with us for a very long time.

Karen was the first to break the silence. She turned to me and said, "I don't know about you Sandrea, but I am finding the atmosphere in this room stifling. I feel like I am struggling to breathe."

"Never mind the atmosphere," Martin added, "is anyone else red hot? Look at me. The sweat is dripping off me!"

As Martin spoke, he wiped his brow and removed his jacket and searched for some place to lay it down. I couldn't help but smile because each of us were unbuttoning and unzipping our coats. Within minutes we had all removed our outer layer of clothing.

I turned back to Karen as I had the sensation that there were many other people sharing this space with us. Though we could not see them physically we sensed their presence. We felt as if we were standing in a very busy underground and people were jostling to try to find or make a personal space. In the silence we could hear the low mumbling of many people communicating with one another.

"Karen, I think you're right," I said. "I feel as if we have been transported back in time, and we are standing in the middle of this room when it was used as a bomb shelter."

"I know," Karen replied. "I keep seeing people pouring down stairs, one after the other, coming into the building. They are all arriving together, but I don't hear the siren."

"It is as if they have come after the siren sounded," Martin said.

"Sandrea, they are everywhere! They are mainly adults, but I can see some small children too," Karen noted.

I began to sink deeply into the vibration to try to understand what was happening here. I knew we were surrounded by lost souls—beings who didn't realize they were dead. As I fine-tuned my psychic senses, I saw a factory nearby with many people caught off guard as the building was destroyed by a incendiary bomb. I wondered if these people had ignored the siren or if the siren had failed to warn them? I had no way of knowing, but what I clearly saw was lots of people wiped out by one bomb—and it appeared this was not the only bomb that had fallen on the area and killed people. Not knowing they were dead, all these spirits still made their way to the safety of the shelter where the presence of the living helped some to recognize their fate and know that their lives were over. They had all become trapped in this confined space and had been there for over fifty years.

We talked together for a while to work out the best strategy of dealing with so many lost souls at one time. The owner watched and listened to us in amazement, but then he, too, was being affected by the stifling atmosphere. He had also removed his coat and rolled up his shirt sleeves.

I tuned in to White Feather to seek his advice. In my mind's eye I saw what must be created—a golden pathway leading to a silver opening. Before I could relay the information of what I was seeing, Karen also said she was viewing the same scene.

I told Karen and the others of the vision White Feather had just given me, and we were all in agreement that we would use the external wall adjacent to the old staircase to create a golden staircase and the silver doorway back to heaven.

We spent a few minutes in silence building the vision. Soon we could see hundreds of the departed standing and waving and welcoming their loved ones home.

Suddenly the spirit of a young girl of about age ten turned to her mother and said, "Mummy, look! Over there! It's Daddy! Can you see? He's waving at us!"

The child was so excited, she was in glee. "Daddy!" she shouted as she began to run up the golden staircase towards her father. The mother also ran up the staircase, and the family was reunited at last.

The team began tuning into the different beings in the room. There must have been over fifty lost souls crammed into this small space. One by one we singled out individuals and pointed out mothers, fathers, husbands, wives, and children. When necessary, we gently urged them to look towards the light. Some had to be nudged along with comforting thoughts. Most needed no prompting, and within ten minutes, these lost ones had left the earth plane and returned to where they belonged in heaven.

Very quickly the space returned to normal. The heaviness began to lift from the room and the emptiness could be felt by all of us. We checked every nook and cranny and corner of the room to ensure no spirit was left behind. We then sealed the silver doorway and the golden staircase slowly disintegrated.

The owner was extremely grateful for our work that night. He shyly admitted that before this evening, he had been quite skeptical to the idea that his cellar may have been haunted and, while he couldn't see the things we did that night, he was convinced he had felt the ghostly presence of souls from a long-ago time.

Multiple Hauntings

Claire had been unable to believe her luck when she collected the keys for her new house. It was exactly what she had wanted—three bedrooms and located close to the school and the public transport service.

Why she had become so lucky would soon become apparent—the place was bursting with paranormal activity.

Within weeks, Claire was desperate and had begun to contact anyone she could think of for help and then she eventually found me. The list of problems she described seemed endless, and I felt exhausted just listening. The singular most frightening thing was a huge, foreboding figure dressed in a monk's cloak that watched her in the living room. The three children were terrified of the stairs, saying that something was chasing them, and when it wasn't chasing them it was watching them. The little boy complained of something "bouncing" off him in the night, and he was now afraid to go into his own room.

Claire noted that her own bedroom appeared to be the hub of the activity. In that room, there was the spirit of a little girl who kept calling to her and asking Claire to be her mommy. Claire was also kept awake by a couple arguing, and she had seen another figure crouching in the corner.

Claire was living in the house with her partner Jonathan. Things had finally come to a head a few days earlier when Jonathan had called his parents in the early hours of the morning, requesting they come over. When the parents arrived, they couldn't believe their eyes when they saw the children asleep on the floor inside a circle of salt.

Lyn, Bill, and I arrived on a warm evening, wearing thin, casual jackets, so we were ill-prepared for the extreme cold that hit us as soon as we walked through the entrance. It was like stepping into a freezer. The icy air seemed to fill the whole house. I pulled my coat closer and zipped it up in an effort to ward off the chilling sensation. I glanced at the fire and all four burners were alight. With Jonathan's parents Sue and Ian present, we all knew we were in for a difficult time.

It was difficult to know where to begin our work as the whole property seemed to be filled with a dark, foreboding, and sinister vibration that was made worse by the penetrating cold. It was so bad, we could all see our breath in the air.

We took time to explain to the family precisely what we were going to do and that we needed them to trust us and to do precisely as we requested without question. The group knew this would be a battle of power—light versus dark, and the only winner had to be the light. In order to do this, we would all have to work as one.

We decided to begin in the living room and found that we didn't have to look far. There in the corner stood a motionless, tall, black-robed figure. Its face was obscured by the hood of the robe. It made no attempt to move but stood perfectly still, as if challenging us to try to defeat it.

I had, in fact, come across this type of demon before, and I knew its power, so I was ready for it. We strategically placed Claire between us as we felt she was the most vulnerable one and that this entity would probably try to seize her at the first opportunity.

Suddenly a loud bang came from the upstairs, as if someone or something had knocked heavily against a door. "Did you hear that?" Claire asked with a nervous edge in her voice.

I nodded my head in agreement. Again came the loud bang.

"What is it?" Claire asked while she clung to Jonathan.

I told her it was something trying to distract us.

The knocking continued for several more minutes. It increased in volume and frequency and then became a series of rapid bangs, almost without any break in between.

I looked at everyone. "It is trying to frighten and distract us, and we must ignore it."

No sooner had I said this than the sound began to subside until it stopped altogether, as if the entity was acknowledging defeat. We turned our attention to this huge, foreboding demon that looked akin to the Angel of Death.

"He's here, isn't he?" Claire asked, pointing her finger at the exact spot.

"Yes, he is," I answered.

Sue, who was smaller in stature than I, looked up at Claire, and then placed her arm around Claire's waist. I could feel the tension increasing in Claire's voice as she spoke.

"Can you see him?" Claire asked.

"We all can," Lyn replied.

"Is it the Grim Reaper?" Claire asked as she looked at the space where the demon stood.

"Something like that," I said.

I then urged Claire and the others not to look at the demon or the area where it stood.

Claire's lovely eyes filled with tears. "Who has he come for? Has he come to take me?"

"He has come for no one, I promise," I said.

The team began to power up in preparation for banishing this demon. We made no attempt to communicate with it or look in its direction. We shielded our third eye, from the demon. The third eye is known as the "eye of insight"; located in the forehead, it is often opened by meditation. Sheilding the third eye was a safety mechanism to avoid the risk of the entity trying to reach us and pull us in. If we fell into its grasp we would be doomed.

We all knew this demon had been summoned, that it was pure evil, and that it was definitely ready for a challenge. It knew our intentions and the danger of it was that it embodied far more power than we could collectively generate—and it could cause serious damage if given half a chance. The battle began.

With us as mere conduits, the other side began their work. First a doorway opened, and the demon almost immediately fell backward through the doorway! As it fell back to its own dimension, a long sliver of dark energy extended across the room—not once or twice but three times—as the demon carefully and deliberately placed slivers of its own vibration onto Claire. By doing this it was establishing a doorway back into our world. The entity was not giving up without a fight.

Instantly Claire felt the dark energy pierce her own aura. "It's on me!" she squealed. "I can feel it! It's on me!"

Lyn scanned from behind Claire and pointed to her right shoulder. At the same time, Bill pointed to her left hip and right ankle.

"Where is it, Claire?" I asked urgently.

"It's on my shoulder!" As Claire spoke she pointed to her right shoulder, precisely where Lyn had indicated.

"I can feel it on my left hip, and it's wrapped around my ankle! Take it away! Take it away!" Claire begged.

We began to generate huge waves of energy to weaken and shift the hold that these slivers of energy had on Claire. After several minutes, we finally managed to clear her of all traces of the entity. The doorway was swiftly shut down and the last of this demon was thrust back to where it came from.

We now headed up the stairs to check the bedrooms. As we walked along we could feel the foreboding energy in every part of the house. It was as if the walls were filled with an evil vibration.

The team decided to start in Jonathan and Claire's bedroom as it was where a lot of the paranormal activity had been taking place. The room was pleasantly decorated, although the black wallpaper with its huge white flowers seemed to actually be encasing a negative vibration.

I have to say that as soon as we entered this room it felt quite full, and this was not at all surprising to any of us, as in total we immediately found four entities in the space. There was an older person crouching by the wardrobe, a man and a woman standing together—whom I suspected were the ones Claire had heard arguing—and finally, there was a little girl with blonde hair who looked pure and innocent, although her face was hidden from us. Lyn was the first to spot the little girl and she began to describe her. As she spoke, Claire shook her head.

"She's not who she says she is! Be careful!" Claire warned us as she choked back tears.

It was now obvious that the little girl had been terrorizing Claire.

We held this child spirit in a very small space. In seconds she turned her head 360 degrees! As it looked at us, the face was hideous with large, yellow eyes set in gray skin. There also appeared to be a hole in the entity's one cheek. It held its face in a sneer, exposing short, black stubs for teeth. Within a few seconds we became aware of the fact that this demon wasn't a female at all, but a male. It was in the bedroom because it had been feeding off the sexual energy. Claire said it kept asking her to do things that were horrible. We were not going to be in the company of this thing for a moment longer.

While lacking the power of the demon in the living room, without a doubt this was still demonic and it had been invited here.

Two demons in the same house—it was extremely rare.

Just then another bang was heard followed by several others. It appeared to be generated from thin air, and the sounds seemed to be coming from halfway down the stairs but not really coming from the stairs. It was just another distraction.

With a doorway opened, the spirit world used their infinite powers to remove the demonic force and return it back to its own world where it could do no harm.

We next concentrated our energies on the male and female. Lyn began to describe what the male looked like while Bill described the female. They both appeared to be under the influence of alcohol. Bill felt that a fire had been the cause of their demise and Claire noted that the male entity had already told her this. As is often the case, these two souls had somehow gotten entangled in the vibrations and energies of the dark forces and had been held captive. Claire warned us to watch the female.

It was the man who was the drinker. The cause of the fire and of their demise had been an unattended frying pan. The large female with her straggly greasy hair was different. She had seen the pain and distress the small demon had caused and she had relished it. In a short period of time she had become its assistant and had joined in tormenting Claire and Jonathan every chance she had. I definitely felt she was ten shades darker than when she had existed in her human form.

We all concentrated our energies on banishing the woman first. She didn't want to go, but she was eventually pulled through the doorway. The man was different; we simply needed to open the doorway and over he hopped. The old man in the corner needed no prompting either, and as soon as the doorway opened he walked through without any further ado. He didn't even look to see who had come for him, because he was so glad to be released from the earth plane.

The next room we entered was a girl's room, decked out in pretty shades of pink. This appeared to be the only room where darkness had not penetrated. We soon became aware of an angelic force in this room, and Claire was able to confirm that the daughters often spoke of an angel looking over them. The girls hated the stairs and the rest of the house, yet once they were in their room they felt safe.

In the bathroom there was a small, dark, and round entity with long hair and red eyes. It was the size of a soccer ball and was hidden in the corner. This entity was something that appeared to be good at generating fear and it was this odd-shaped entity that had tormented the little boy. This entity was quickly banished.

Our final point of focus was the staircase where half-way up it appeared there was an opening or doorway to another dimension. Together we quickly closed it down, ensuring that nothing would ever venture out of this dark space again.

We spent a great deal of time removing all traces of the negative vibrations from the very fabric of the house. To our eyes the walls appeared stained by the darkness. We utilized every tool we could. Working systematically, we sent waves and spirals of energy, we bounced balls of light off the walls to remove trapped negative energy and cleaned the corners where the dark vibrations seemed to hang. While we had worked in this house now for quite a while it was in the final five minutes that the place began to feel warmer and lighter. Yet, even though we had come this far, we all knew it was going to take a little more to get this property straight. The dark purple and gaudy red colors that covered the walls seemed to hold onto the remnants of the negative energy. It was going to take lighter colors to return this house to normalcy. We acknowledged we had done all we could and that the final stages would be up to the homeowners to remove these colors from the walls.

By the end of the evening, Sue and Ian had their perspectives changed. They had witnessed for themselves the cold, the bolts of fear, and the loud bangs. Without a doubt, these demonic forces had been invited in by a former tenant and Claire and Jonathan were mere victims of circumstance, because the darkness had simply carried on to them.

While the problems never returned, I did hear that Claire and Jonathan moved out about a year later.

The house was clear, but the memories lived on.

House for Rent, Partly Occupied

Beth had moved into a new apartment with her beloved dogs and things had been fine until a couple of months ago when she began to feel very uncomfortable in the living room and bedroom. Even the dogs were at times reluctant to enter these two rooms and seemed to prefer lying close to the front door, as if trying to avoid something. The little dog had also begun to bark constantly— something it had never done before—and the situation had now reached a point where Beth could not leave the dogs alone on the property for fear the incessant barking would anger the neighbors.

Further, Beth noted there were often cold spots, obnoxious smells, and the sensation of being watched. She had also seen orbs in two of the rooms and the ghost of an old lady in the kitchen.

Feeling we could manage this one, Martin and I went to Beth's alone.

Oddly, for some reason our guides wanted Beth off the property, and we reluctantly requested that she leave while we checked out her house.

No sooner had we arrived than we detected a strong male presence. We knew this entity was the root cause of all the issues facing Beth. This was a very arrogant man. He stayed well away from Martin, but at every opportunity he tried to attack me. First he attempted to frighten me by appearing either directly in front of me or behind me and then disappearing very quickly. He also tried to intimidate me by coming as close as he possibly could. I must admit that the combination of his speed and closeness did unnerve me a bit.

Martin and I moved to the bedroom to begin our work when suddenly I felt the entity materialize to my left side. He moved incredibly close to me and I could feel his hot, rancid breath near my ear. I could also feel the fear he was bombarding me with. I maintained a guarded demeanor and ignored the entity.

Martin looked at me and we both smiled at one another, because Martin could see what this spirit was doing and he also knew of my plan to undermine him.

But the spirit was also causing Martin a great deal of trouble as he cloaked himself and shifted and darted around in order to avoid detection. Martin was using a lot of his psychic energy to pin down the location of this entity.

It soon became apparent why we had been compelled to ask Beth to leave the apartment—all our energy would have gone to trying to protect her. With only half the team here, we would have been in a weakened state. With her away from the premises, we could concentrate on the matter at hand.

It was difficult for us to determine information about this spirit, for example, had he once lived in this apartment or had be once resided in an adjacent house? Without a doubt he had connections to this block. However, whether he had lived in the apartment or another building close by, walls are no barriers to spirits, so he could easily slip from one property to the other. Of course he could not do this anymore as we had the apartment tightly sealed. That didn't stop him from moving from room to room as he dodged Martin and did whatever he could to unnerve me. I did not show an ounce of fear that night, but believe me, I felt it. Every time the spirit did something to spook me, I felt it in my solar plexus and booted it right back out again.

Twenty minutes later, we were still searching for him. It was as if we were playing a game of hide-and-seek—or in this case hide-and-attack.

Martin decided the only way to deal with this entity was to offer it his energy field and entice the spirit into his aura. Martin would then be reliant on me and the other side to remove the entity. This definitely felt like the proper course of action, so we decided to lure the entity into Martin's energy field. Then the guides and I would move the entity on.

We spent a few moments tuning in and finding out a little bit about this spirit man and the information was not exactly good. It would appear that he had lived his life without spiritual influence—drinking, taking drugs, and encouraging young teenage girls to come into his apartment. He appeared to not have worked for years and he had given very little back to the world. He was a self-server, looking after himself to the exclusion of anyone else. Considering the manner in which he had lived his life it was no wonder he was reluctant to move from this world. In fact, it was the fear that held him prisoner in this vibration. He had learned very little in the ten years since his passing, and he was still using his will in a negative sense, tormenting any female he came into contact with.

Beth was by no means the first—the difference with Beth was that she had psychic ability and was able to differentiate between herself and external interference. Now that we understood what we were up against, we could begin the process.

Martin stood silently with his eyes closed and his energy field open and inviting. His arms were slightly out to the side, portraying an invitation, and his head was resting on his chest to avoid conflict. The temptation was too much and, of course, our spirit could not resist.

I waited until the entity's vibration was fully tuned with Martin. In fact, as I watched I could actually see the point when the spirit stepped into Martin's energetic field. It took a few moments to adjust and then Martin appeared to grow broader and taller by about three to four inches. When Martin raised his head, a five o'clock shadow overlay his clean-shaven face, and his eyes appeared much darker and quite sinister. The spirit looked at me and I looked back. It could not believe its luck! It had a body and it was going to use it. I could feel the hatred and all the emotions associated with darkness pouring from Martin towards me and hitting me like small, dark arrows. This entity tried to force its will upon me as best it could. It adjusted Martin's posture, his chin jutted out, and he held Martin's lips together tightly. His eyes never left my face and he used his piercing gaze to increase the fear. But its ill desire would be its downfall.

Embedded well into Martin's energetic field, the entity had full use of this body to do as he pleased, but this body was also his prison. He knew he was trapped. Before he realized what he had done, the etheric world sprang into action and began the work of blasting the entity from Martin's energetic field back to its own dimension. I could feel the bewilderment the spirit was experiencing.

Martin began to move from side to side, darting his head as the entity tried to find a way out. But it was too late. The doorway was open and the other side pushed relentlessly for a few minutes. In no time at all he was gone, banished back to the spirit world.

As if by magic, a nervous Beth called from the door to see if it was okay to come in. Martin went to the door and let her enter.

"Oh my God, what have you done?" she said as her hand flew to her mouth in total surprise. "I cannot believe the difference! Have you changed the light bulbs and turned the heating up?"

Martin and I stood there smiling and shook our heads as we both said "no" in unison.

We explained that we had done nothing but clear the apartment as we had promised.

We then went on to tell Beth what we had encountered and the reason why she had been asked to leave. She listened and she understood.

Then she asked, "Wasn't there a lady in the kitchen?"

We had forgotten about her! With the dark entity out of the way we could now explore this with Beth. We all moved to the kitchen to try to determine who or what she had encountered in there. Martin and I decided that since Beth had been denied the privilege of seeing her tormentor banished, we would work with her when we found the old lady spirit in the kitchen.

Within a very few moments, Beth told us who she thought the spirit in the kitchen was. She believed it was her grandmother's sister Nancy. She had passed over long ago when Beth was a small child, yet Beth could remember her and had fond memories of this lady. There was no need for us to clear this spirit as we found that Nancy had come to Beth's rescue.

Edwardian Mansion

Following a terrible flood in the summer of 2008, a close friend Steve had found temporary accommodations in a converted former mansion in Staffordshire. Set on half an acre of wooded and landscaped gardens, it was idyllic and perfectly fit with his lifestyle. While one couldn't help but admire the splendor of the property, it had an uncomfortable air about it, and from the odd occasions I visited I was able to sense something else in residence.

There was no real way to define what I felt when I visited Steve, because I couldn't put my finger on it exactly— the only way to say it was that things didn't feel right.

During a recent visit I had the strangest encounter.

While I was standing in the bedroom of the apartment a small hole opened in the ether directly in front of me and a strange mist began to surround the hole. Through the hole a miniature man appeared. He stood with his hands on his hips and surveyed his surroundings but did not notice me. Physically he appeared to be about eight inches tall and he had long, brown curly hair and a fancy moustache. He was dressed in a deep-red suit from a long ago time, and a sword was on a belt around his waist. This odd being only stayed for a few minutes, then promptly stepped back through the hole, and the entire scene vanished as quickly as it had appeared. I couldn't wait to tell Paul about the experience.

A few days later I stood at the bottom of the stairs, admiring the lavish staircase. I slowly became aware of a very angry male spirit to my right. He was dressed in eighteenth-century finery of beige breeches, black jacket, and white shirt. He was totally unaware of me and was angrily kicking at the wall. When I took a closer look, I could see there had once been a doorway in that spot. I was unsure whether he was kicking the wall because it blocked his path or whether this was something he had done when he was in physical form.

This was no hologram—this was a lost soul—a ghost haunting his former abode.

I continued to watch from a distance and made the decision not to try to communicate with him until I had other people with me.

As I slipped out of the hallway, he was still kicking and lashing out and I was rather glad that Steve's apartment location was not in the pathway of this spirit.

A while later, Steve decided to go away for a few days. While he was away he thought the daughter of one of his friends might like to stay in the apartment and, considering the location, she had apparently jumped at the opportunity.

During her first night there the woman was awakened numerous times by the video entrance phone that linked the apartment to the electronic gates, but no one was there to give entrance to. On the second night, and desperate for a good night's sleep, she left the device muted. At around three in the morning she was abruptly awakened to the sound of scurrying in the bathroom adjoining the bedroom, which lasted for about forty-five minutes.

The final straw came when she returned one day to find her clothes strewn across the bedroom and her belongings tossed around the living room. She promptly packed her things and left.

Steve gave my team permission to investigate, so my team and I gathered at Steve's place. Besides me, the team consisted of Chris and John, a husband-and-wife team who are both pyschics and mediums; Stella, a gifted psychic I've worked with for many years; and Karen and Martin.

We were concerned there could be more lost souls trapped in this building other than the angry wall-kicking spirit, and if this was the case we were going to offer assistance to help them on their way. Going into this we knew it was not going to be easy: first, we didn't have the permission of the other tenants to clear the building on their behalf, and second, we only had access to a very limited part of the building. These things would limit what we could do—nevertheless, we decided to push on anyway and try to clear what we could.

As soon as we had all arrived we began to explore the public portion of the grand house. Like me, everyone felt a strong presence on the stairs. As we ascended, a wilted balloon tied to the upper balcony gave a sinister appearance. It was almost as if it represented someone hanging from the spindles. This thought was shared by several of us and, in fact, the image we got was of a limp female body hanging from the balustrade. From the group image we shared we built up a picture, which affirmed that at least one person, possibly female, had hanged herself in this vicinity.

We also searched the deserted entertainment rooms in the basement and found them to have an extremely depressive effect on all of us. A large room held a full-sized billiards table, chairs, and plenty of room to move about. However, the entertainment factor of the room did nothing to change how people felt during their time in the space, because the majority of those present complained of finding it difficult to breathe; some had the onset of headaches that made it feel as if their heads were in a vise. The atmosphere here was just too suppressive and intense for us to work comfortably, so we decided that we would attempt to clear this area from Steve's apartment.

We headed back to Steve's, trying to be as quiet as possible so that we didn't disturb the other occupants. We were walking along the corridor when Karen stopped and tapped on the wall molding. Stella was directly behind Karen, and when she reached the spot where Karen had tapped, she heard a gentle tapping sound, as if the rail was tapping back. Stella casually mentioned the tapping to everyone. We all returned to the spot and gently tapped on the molding; the tap came back to us as an immediate response.

We moved onto the apartment and arranged ourselves in a circle; we began to tune in to see what we could pick up. Previously we had dimmed the lights so we could still see movement in the room; however, the light was not so bright that it would impair our psychic senses. It wasn't long before the atmosphere of the room began to change.

The hairs on the backs of our necks felt as if they were standing on end and there was no apparent reason for this—yet each of us reported the same sensation. Next, we all complained of churning stomachs and an element of intense fear entering the space. As in the basement, several of us reported difficulty breathing as the intensity of the atmosphere continued to grow.

As our eyes began to acclimate to the reduced light, the room suddenly began to grow even darker and then darker still. We could psychically see the light in the room fading. It was as if some unseen and prevailing wind had brought in a dark cloud. This dark cloud appeared to encompass the whole room. It entered in by the living room door and exited out the opposite external wall. Contained within this shadow was a stream of entities flowing into the room—male, female, young, old—all in different styles of dress. At one point, I felt we were being overwhelmed by the stream of ghosts as more and more drifted into the room encased in this ominous cloud.

As the light level fell, we all commented on it, as it was so profound. Even Paul, who claimed to have no psychic gifts, agreed with us. The room became darker and darker and the atmosphere seemed to increase in density. Some of us saw entities, some saw orbs, and others just felt the change.

As the dark cloud, entities, and orbs flowed around us, Karen spoke a split second before I could. "Sandrea, I can feel lots and lots of beings entering the room. They do not belong here, but somehow at the point of death they became trapped here."

I agreed and so did several others. It was clear that some of the spirits did not realize they were now without physical bodies. Others appeared trapped and unable to find a way out of this Edwardian prison. As we sat and watched, it was as if some unseen being was guiding them—herding them into the living room in droves. Through the dim light we could psychically see a stream of ghosts aimlessly walking about in a circle with no place to go. There were now so many in the room it seemed it was impossible any more could fit. I had never experienced anything like this before; it was like a scene out of a horror movie as the spirits continued walking about in utter silence.

No words were spoken for a while as we tried to comprehend what was happening here. Personally I felt overcome by the situation and soon a frightened, sinking feeling overtook me as I began to consider that this time we may have bitten off more than we could chew!

I silently spoke to White Feather and Quan Yin and expressed my fears of not knowing how to deal with the situation.

Karen broke into my thoughts. "Sandrea, I can see a golden gate." As I focused, I could see the golden arched gate she spoke about slowly opening.

"Are the gates arched?" I asked.

"Yes," Karen replied.

This was all the confirmation I needed and there was solace in knowing we were both seeing the same thing.

"We need to send our energy to these spirit people to guide them through the gates," Karen said.

"Okay, let's do it. Let's send positive vibrations towards the gates to encourage them to go through." And we did just that.

Telepathically we communicated with some of the spirits and reassured them this was the way to go. For about fifteen minutes we created positive energy to help and guide. Spirits continued to flow into the room and it was as if we had opened a doorway from purgatory and these lost souls came through as they shifted from one world to another; we were the bridge facilitating this. It was impossible to count how many spirits streamed through that golden gateway, but slowly the flow became a trickle. I did notice that the angry, kicking ghost from downstairs also passed through and I was glad of that. Finally one or two stragglers made the transition from one dimension to the other. There were a few reluctant ones who tried to stay behind, but we connived, cajoled, and finally managed to get them through. At the moment there was nothing left, but we waited for a few minutes to make sure. I saw the gates slowly begin to diminish.

"I think it's over," I said.

Martin was a bit more empathic. "I know. They have just closed the gate."

At the same time a lighter energy began to pour into the room. Stella commented about seeing the golden color, and we all agreed with her. The energy appeared to run across the room and out the door. We didn't know how far it extended, because we were all still amazed by what we had just witnessed.

With the last of the stragglers back in their own world, our work was seemingly completed, and we all managed a huge sigh of relief that it had gone so well and was hopefully over.

Later, while we sat sharing a bite to eat, we wondered—why had so many spirits become trapped in one area? We contemplated numerous causes for this trapping of these lost souls on the earth plane. It would take a while before we had the answers.

Karen, Martin, Steve, and I returned on two occasions to continue with the work at the mansion. We psychically swept the building as we tried to send over any remaining wandering souls. We went back down to the basement and opened a one-way door to encourage the flow. We also meditated together in the house to try to understand precisely what had happened here and what had caused these spirits to become trapped. We were given to understand that the house had been placed on a major node. This is what had caused it to become a trap, preventing wandering souls from making their final transition.

No doubt there are throughout our land many other places like the Edwardian mansion that have been built on sacred sites and are places where lost souls become trapped in the very fiber of the building.

Eight

More Haunted Places

There are some sites that should never be built upon and these stories tell of the ghostly ones who died of smallpox years and years ago and remained tied to the place of their deaths. There is also another dragon demon and a dark presence in a home that is situated on the site of an ancient priory.

Land Not to Be Built Upon

Lindsey was an extremely gifted, natural medium who lived in the country in a large and spacious barn conversion. The barn sat in the midst of several other conversions close to a mansion.

The land was rich in history. The first recorded activity was a Roman fort, then a monastery until the Dissolution, and then a convent that remained active for a few centuries until the 1700s.

Lindsey's house was not the only one to be subjected to paranormal disturbances. Lindsey was able to sense some of the spirits residing in her home and she knew the ones to acknowledge and the ones to stay clear of.

Lindsey and her husband Rich had been living in the house for about two years, and from the beginning they had been subjected to what can only be described as an array of abnormal incidents and episodes. The events were not exclusive to the family, as guests would invariably be awakened in the middle of the night to the sound of the fitted wardrobe doors opening and closing. This phenomenon was usually accompanied by coat hangers clattering together as if a blast of wind had passed through the room—and the activity was not limited to one particular bedroom, because it spread throughout all five of the bedrooms. Lindsey had once caught her youngest child applying blue shelving paper to the extensive range of cupboards and wardrobes in his room. When she gently inquired what he was doing, he told her, "Mommy the doors keep opening and closing at night, and it wakes me up."

After I heard about the things going on in Lindsey's home I definitely felt a visit was necessary and soon descended on the house with some of the more advanced members of my group from the spiritualist church. In the future they would be called upon to do this type of work so they needed a practical lesson. I also had Linda, Paul, and Bill with me so I had sufficient power, but the assistance of four other mediums would be an added bonus.

We all swooped into Lindsey's home one cold November evening. It didn't matter that we had a big group because the home was of a size where everyone could fit in any of the rooms with space left over. The house was incredibly large and consisted of two living rooms, a dining room and kitchen, with another dining area set in the hallway. On the first floor were five bedrooms and three bathrooms. Of the two living rooms, one was rarely used. As we moved through the place, we noted that the only room not affected by anything negative was the kitchen. It was interesting to note this was where the family cats preferred to stay most of the time.

The major feature of the home was its impressive hallway, and it was only later that we would realize how important the area was.

The room where the television was located was the most popular place in the house, yet Lindsey's husband didn't like this space at all.

"Where does he sit when he is in here?" I asked.

Lindsey gestured to a chair by a window that was across the room.

I began to sense a huge, dark and menacing presence behind the chair. I didn't say a word to anyone because the group needed to find the ghostly presence on their own.

They walked around the room, soaking up the atmosphere. I stayed in control but at the same time gave the others space to hone their skills. As my team and I watched, the church group members were drawn to the area behind Rich's chair. They felt there was something in the area.

I could clearly see a figure in a dark-gray hooded cloak who stood about 6'6" tall and was faceless. His appearance was akin to that of the Grim Reaper; the only difference was that he carried no scythe in his hand. He was extremely daunting, and a very menacing energy surrounded him.

"What is directly above here?" I asked as I pointed towards the ceiling.

"One of the children's bedrooms," Lindsey replied.

"Let's start upstairs," I said, motioning towards the door.

We all went up the stairs and worked our way through the various rooms and landings until we reached the room directly above the television room—but the entity was already here. He stood motionless in the corner just watching with a faceless stare—menacing unseen eyes from underneath his hood tracking us. I could feel the power of this being and knew it was far greater than us and could easily overpower us.

The group moved in between the bathroom and bedroom as they tried to decide where to start. All the time the entity stood silently observing. As we walked around the two rooms, I sensed White Feather draw in very close.

He was strongly urging me to have nothing to do with this malign force and to stay well away from it.

This was one of those times when I facilitated exiling a malevolent force without some sort of inter-communication between me and it. I gave clear instructions to all to attempt no psychic connections to the entity.

And as for me I needed no further prompting from White Feather.

I could sense this entity was from the darkest side of hell and was much too strong for ordinary earthlings to attempt a banishment. Mentally we now began to build a golden wall of light around the far corner where the evil being stood. We took several moments to complete this. As soon as the task was done the room began to fill with beings of light as several large, golden angels swept into the space.

The other side meant business and they had sent the best to execute this task.

The angelic ones boxed the entity in on three sides and walked forward, creating a wall of energy. In doing so, the entity was forced through a darkened doorway that had appeared behind him. The pathway in front of him was blocked and we were protected. The only way out was backwards into the hole and that's exactly where he went, back to his own dimension.

Satisfied that the worst of the beings in the home had been dealt with, and safe in the knowledge he was truly ensconced in hell once more, we could move on. Each member of the group had, in one way or the other, witnessed the transporting of the entity back to its own dimension. As validation, they either described the force that pulled the being through the doorway, the size of the evil being, or the terrible negativity that pervaded the area where he had stood.

Next came the boy's bedroom, which was joined by a bathroom sandwiched between the two rooms. In here we felt the main problem had been the hooded being, but we still wanted to ensure all the rooms were cleared of any residual energy. Together we pushed a thick, solid wall of white light from one room to the other to clear the place of negativity. We then placed miniature tornadoes around the house to try to freshen the atmosphere that still hung in a thick, menacing manner. As usual, the effect was almost instantaneous and the rooms appeared much lighter.

We now went across the landing to the parent's bedroom and as we did so we could feel the power beneath our feet. The farther we walked, the greater it became. The power here was all-encompassing and I began to suspect there were several issues here. Not only were there more ghostly phenomena to deal with, but there was a build-up of destructive vibrations. The final issue was the fact that the house was sitting on a key ley line and right here in the middle of the hallway was a major node, or cross-over point. Now our focus was on the master bedroom.

As we entered this big and beautiful room, we could all sense the presence of other beings. Again I let the group decide who or what was here, and they all worked for quite a while establishing that there was an ethereal imprint covering a section of the space. It would seem there had been an outbreak of smallpox in the area in the distant past and many people, both young and older, had gathered here and died. It was not a hospital, per se—it felt more like a gathering place. People had brought their sick here, hoping for a miracle. Also, by removing the dying from their homes they had hoped to save the living. There were many, many lost souls here, trapped in the vibration of this hellhole, held by the fear and misery of that time period.

We created a doorway through to the other side but these disembodied spirits had been here for so long that they shied away from the brightness of the light. We then mentally adjusted the brightness of the doorway to a lower level and this made the portal more appealing and inviting to them. We gently moved and manipulated the energy until we held these wretched lost souls in a circle of the dull light. As they moved towards the portal, we stepped back and allowed the other side to do their work. Soon one spirit edged nervously towards the portal, followed by the rest. In tota,l we saw twelve souls cross over that night. It should be noted that we had merely created a gateway and that not all of these spirits had resided in Lindsey and Rich's bedroom.

One spirit stood out to us—a little boy of about eight who was separate from the wretched crowd. Looking at his face, I could clearly see that he had been a victim of this horrible disease and had not survived. It felt as if somehow he had become trapped in our world.

The little boy had been communicating with Lindsey for some time now, chatting with her and keeping her company when her husband was away at work. The little boy was not alone.

There was a woman with the boy and she was not his mother. She gave the impression of someone similar to a nurse—a woman who had been watching over the child. This woman preferred to stay in the shadows and, from the bumps on her face, it appeared that she had also been a smallpox victim.

As Lindsey had formed quite a bond with the boy, she didn't really want him to go, but he did not belong here. He belonged back in the spirit world where he had family of his own. After a short discussion, Lindsey reluctantly agreed to let go of the boy. We then built a wall of white light, created a doorway, and helped him through. Quite soon we could all feel the presence of a wonderful soft-pink energy and sensed that several cherubic angels had come to help lift the child over the veil. He was closely followed by his nursemaid. When they had gone, we sealed the room with a vibrant flow of energy and set off to tackle the other rooms.

Another large living room was directly below Lindsey's bedroom, so anything paranormal that happened upstairs percolated downstairs. All that remained to be done in this space was to re-vibrate the ether. The ground had been belching black spirals of energy into the room, and it clung to the very fiber of the space. We felt the problem amplified by the presence of stagnant water that probably lay deep down in the earth below the foundation. We spent time walking walls of energy from one side of the room to the other, reinvigorating it. This was repeated a couple of times. Although it was quite exhausting, our efforts were repaid immediately with a feeling of calm and contentment. Now we felt we were almost done.

All that remained was the hall, stairs, and landing.

Lindsey told us that the previous night the eldest son had woken in the night to the sound of marching soldiers. From his bed, he had watched a mass of these men in red and white uniforms running up the stairs. Some had been on the stairs and others were above it, and still others had run straight through the walls. The son reported that the men moved at quick marching speed with bayonets fixed, indicating active conflict. As they marched, the boy could clearly hear the beating of a drum. The youngster had seen and heard the whole event, which he stated had lasted around three to four minutes.

As quickly as the marching soldiers appeared, the scene faded in front of his eyes.

Julie, a member of the spiritualist church, said she felt there was a huge opening in the hallway by the staircase at exactly the point where I had felt it upstairs. Everyone else was in agreement. There was definitely some type of hole in this area. Another member of the church, Sue, then piped up and said there was a line running off it. I knew immediately we had a huge node set in the middle of the staircase, a doorway through to the other side.

Realizing what we were up against, we began the process of dealing with it. It was one very tired group of people who made one final effort and began to close off the node. Together we imagined a huge slab of granite stone plugging the hole. Then we called upon our guides to help us seal it. We then tried to mentally push the line so that it would be diverted outside of the building.

Two and a half hours later we all set off in different directions, satisfied we had, at least for the time being, made the property a better place to live.

Without a doubt, nothing should ever have been built on this land and for several reasons. First, because of the node that sat directly underneath the house—but more importantly because of the poignant events that had taken place on this ground over several centuries. The monastery, the hospital, and the convent had all made their mark on the land. Hundreds of years of history could not be wiped out by a group of mediums. While we had managed to clear out and shift a lot of psychic debris, there was still an awful lot left.

As we set off I caught sight of an adjacent property and sensed another hooded figure inside the house. This one was more powerful than the one we had removed from Lindsey's home.

Despite their grandeur, I was very glad I was not living in one of these homes.

Dragon's Den

Lily came to me for a private reading and towards the end of it I became aware that something was seriously wrong with her home.

Lily explained that she and her boyfriend had lived in the small apartment for five years. During that time they had been subjected to many different incidents but somehow didn't manage to fathom that the problems were with the apartment. One scary occurrence happened when a huge wardrobe toppled onto their bed during the night. Thankfully they escaped injury. Lily said this wardrobe was so heavy it took several people to lift it back up. No one could find any logical reason for this wardrobe to have fallen.

Other unexplainable things that happened included water pipes bursting with increasing regularity despite the fact that most of the pipes had been replaced. The dehumidifiers ran constantly, yet they could not combat the damp atmosphere, and water ran down the windows and walls, taking off the wallpaper. The heating ran constantly, yet the cold penetrated every corner of the place. Lily's boyfriend Tom was pushed down the steps on a regular basis every time he entered the bathroom, and the push was with such force that he would land several feet away. Tom also was now suffering—with increasing regularity—stabbing pains in the middle of his back and chronic stomach aches. All of this was overshadowed by the unnerving feeling that their every move was being watched.

The team and I decided to investigate and we arrived one night in the middle of a storm. Lyn, Kevin, Paul, and I were all soaking wet by the time we reached the front door of the apartment, which was located to the side of a large Edwardian house now converted to apartments.

We noted that several of the apartments were vacant and, according to Lily, no one stayed very long. There were eight apartments in total, and it seemed anyone who had ever lived there was dogged with bad luck or ill health—in some cases a combination of the two. Lily noted that the tenant who lived in the apartment above theirs had been there a bit longer than she and Tom had, and he had been taken out by ambulance recently and never returned.

The group and I noticed immediately the apartment inside felt as cold as it was outside. The dampness hit us as soon as we entered into the small kitchen. The bright colors throughout the tiny three-roomed place did nothing to lift the heavy and dense atmosphere. It seemed hard to understand how this couple had managed to live here all this time in such a negative vibration.

We decided to begin in the single bedroom as it appeared to be the heart of the activity. We moved around the room, searching for the cause of this mayhem. The energy felt so dense we could hardly breathe.

Soon we all began to sense an energy in the right corner alongside where Lily slept. There, standing ominously, was what could only be described as a dragon. It was a huge, malevolent force that dominated the whole space. Once it realized we had tuned into it, this black, evil force unleashed its venom. It turned its attention to us, specifically seeking out Lyn and me. In a split second I felt a deep, stabbing pain between my shoulder blades that made it feel like a red-hot rod was being forced into my body. Simultaneously, Lyn felt a bolt of energy hit her in the stomach as violent cramps ripped through her body. At that precise moment, the energy in the room became charged with fear as this thing swiftly deployed a variety of techniques to overthrow us. Paul and Kevin turned their attention to Lyn and me and used their healing skills to alleviate our pains and discomfort. Again we were up against something that was far greater in power than us mere mortals.

As always, we were to be the conduits for the other side.

We shielded ourselves from the violence of this evil being and began simultaneously to create a portal. Then, and in an effort to push it through the gate, we mentally threw sheets of energy over to the area where this ominous entity stood.

The temperature in the room took a further dip. Positive energy passed across the room and then there seemed to be an incredible rush as the energy darted around the beast. Within seconds it began to fade away as it was slowly pushed and pulled backwards through the huge doorway that took it back to its own dimension. The instant the beast was gone the room began to grow warmer and brighter.

Lily exclaimed, "Oh my goodness! Is that my imagination? It seems so bright in here all of the sudden!"

We could all feel the lifting of the oppressive atmosphere in the room.

With the dragon gone, we then placed tornadoes of energy around the room to remove the remaining strands and shards of darkness.

Next we went into the living room and then the kitchen again. Both of these rooms appeared to be free from further disembodied entities, although the energy still remained dense and foreboding. I turned to look towards the sofa and could not believe my eyes! There, about three feet off the floor, was a concentration of energy and light. Strands and twists of energy turned in and out in a complex pattern. This thing covered an area of three feet or more. It was not a doorway into another world but seemed more like a wormhole that turned back onto itself. I was warned by my guides to handle this with care as we would need to close it at a precise moment when the energies were moving in a certain way. If this wormhole wasn't handled correctly, we would trap this force in our universe and it would cause untold problems for the other side and for anyone who resided in this space.

We could all see this thing turning and spinning and fading in and out as it bridged the two dimensions. In preparation for the actual event, I was shown several times the point when it should be closed off. I was to seal the space when the pattern disappeared.

One, two, three, go!

I heard the countdown in my head and with a mighty mental push, the space was wiped clean and the space where the energy had been seeping through was closed off. We had succeeded, and it was gone forever.

Satisfied we had cleansed and removed any malign forces from the apartment and the remainder of the house, we got ready to leave. I felt urged to turn to Lily and Tom and advise them to find another apartment and move. I felt the memories of this place would always be tarnished for them and their relationship would fare much better when they were away from here. They both acknowledged they had had enough and were actively looking to move elsewhere.

We bid our goodbyes and ran through the relentless rain to our respective cars. As I turned the car to leave,

I caught a glimpse of a huge ley line running towards the house where the apartment was. Ley lines can space twenty feet into the air and be twelve feet wide. I normally perceive them as clouds or sheets of color, which fade in and out as they oscillate. The color will depend on whether the line is negative or positive. Purple is negative and indigo is positive. The ley line I saw in front of me would account for some of the energy found inside. I had to wonder as I drove off—what had happened in that flat in the past to evoke such an evil force? Was it the land the house stood on, or had someone in the once-beautiful place called in this malign force?

We would never know.

Ancient Ground

I was out with some friends sitting in the Wombourne Tandoori Restaurant. We were there for over two hour-seating great food and enjoying one another's company. Some time during the meal, the conversation had turned to my spiritual occupation. Thankfully, my work colleagues have always been open-minded to all esoteric matters and over the years we have shared many a lively discussion on the topic.

During dinner, the subject of the atmosphere in Alison's house arose several times. I treated the comments very lightly at first, yet as the discussion progressed, I began to realize that the matter was not as simple as I had first thought. I began to consider that Alison might actually require help. All the others said they had never felt comfortable in Alison's home. Apparently, no one could relax there and although no one present could put their finger on it, they sensed something was amiss.

Alison also spoke of intrusive dreams—not physically intrusive—she just felt like she was being watched in the night and that someone was trying to talk to her. That someone did not feel nice. What bothered Alison the most was the effect on her youngest daughter Keera, who was now having nightmares and was afraid of being upstairs in any area except her own bedroom. Alison's son also refused to sleep in the front bedroom and the older daughter complained of being watched whenever she was upstairs. Despite the house being less than twelve years old, the inside of the curtains in Alison's bedroom were continually covered in mold. Extensive tests found no sign or evidence of dampness anywhere in the building and yet the mold continued to grow.

After hearing this story I made arrangements to visit the following Monday.

When Karen, Martin, and I arrived we were amazed when we felt the energy outside the front door. It felt vibrant and wild, as if we were all standing on a high ridge. It was quite invigorating and we were amazed that no one apart from us had noticed it enough to mention it.

The house was a beautiful one. Delving into the history of the area it was noted that the small housing complex was believed to have been set on the grounds of an old priory, even though the priory and its remains were long gone. No one seemed to know precisely where the priory had stood and there were no records of its exact location, but there was a plaque dedicated to it on the outskirts of the estate.

It should be noted that far back in history people understood the energy grid that encompasses our planet, and it is believed that the Druids/Pagans placed their sacred sites on strategic energy points. As an act of dominance, early Christians destroyed these structures and built their churches on top of them. This is why many old churches have been mapped as sitting on these sacred lines. The outcome is that these buildings harness the most wonderful energies. While a lot of good energy is created by years of prayer and generating good vibrations, it is also magnified by the location.

From the energy outside the front door of Alison's home we were beginning to form the idea there may very well be one of these major energy grid lines running through this property.

After we went inside, we decided to commence upstairs as this was where the majority of the problems had manifested. We began to systematically walk around the bedrooms and found problems in all four of them, with some rooms worse than others. What was more amazing was that we found different situations in each of the rooms. The only room that seemed to be free of trouble was the house bathroom.

Karen spoke first. "I'm not sure what is going on here, Sandrea, but I have a being that is about three feet tall."

"Yes, I have him," added Martin.

"He has a lot of hair, and I do mean a lot of hair," Karen added.

I was also aware of the entity, but before I could speak Alison confirmed what Karen and Martin had said and added that the entity's hair was an odd shade of brown.

Alison's description of the entity was exactly what we were all seeing.

At first this entity could have been mistaken for being rather sweet, but he was anything but. He was exactly as described and absolutely covered in hair that was brown with a shade of auburn, and the hair stood off his head. He was so unkempt, it was difficult to ascertain where his beard started and his hair ended.

I also became aware of a vortex of energy located on the landing and what could only be described as a stagnant energy sitting underneath the house.

It was now becoming apparent to me that the house was most likely located on a very important ley line, or more importantly, the house was located on a node—and this was a major one. The node was creating a doorway to another dimension; hence this rather belligerent entity had been allowed to cross over from one world to another. He wasn't exactly evil but neither was he an angel. He was just a different energy and vibration to our world.

Realizing we were not here to wish him well, the entity tried to beat a hasty retreat. Unfortunately for him, we had anticipated this and temporarily closed off his exit. For now, he was trapped here until we worked out how to seal the doorway after he had departed.

Very soon the atmosphere in the room began to change as the being realized we had trapped him in this dimension. Our job now was to lose this doorway and ensure he was returned to the world he had come from.

The prayers and protection had created a nice vibration, but this soon began to change as the air became charged. At this point, my solar plexus contracted as the darts of angry rays he threw out bounced around the room, hitting all of us. He tried to aim all his venom at Alison, but we had wrapped her in a mental blanket of light.

Karen yelled out, "Sandrea, this thing is very menacing! I think we should assist him now!"

As Karen spoke she winced in pain and grabbed at her back. Martin looked at me and urged me to start. Like me, he could sense we couldn't hold this entity much longer and the entity was beginning to physically hurt us.

Completely ignoring the entity's outbursts, I guided Alison to state her intention that she no longer wanted the being in her world. When we got her permission, we re-opened the doorway. The entity was kicking and screaming as we gently pushed him back to the dimension where he belonged and then we immediately sealed and capped the doorway to avoid re-entry.

We then mentally opened another doorway and collected the energy in from every corner of the room until it folded in on itself like a collapsible box, and that was pushed through the doorway.

The next room we went into was the study. Very little furniture was in there apart from a couple of wall cabinets and a desk. As we walked around, Martin noted that the energies here were quite stifling. We all began to tune in.

After a few minutes Karen spoke, "I cannot pick anything up."

We all agreed, but the energy just didn't feel right. In fact, it was downright uncomfortable. It would appear that the entity had formed a wall of stagnant vibration, which surrounded the room. It was this heavy vibration that had disturbed Alison's son and driven him from the room. This entity may not have been able to put itself in every room at one time, but it had been able to leave this stagnant pool of negative energy that made it very uncomfortable to be in the room.

We next went to the two rear bedrooms. The energy around the outside of Keera's room felt quite uncomfortable and stifling—different from the front bedroom but uncomfortable nonetheless. However, the energy did not appear to enter the room. To Alison this made sense, as most of the time it was getting in and out of the bedroom that was the problem. Once Keera was in bed, she was fine. Alison told us that on a regular basis Keera talked about the monster that came into her room and looked at her. While the entity had been removed, the energy hadn't, so again we worked at removing and replacing the energy in the space.

As we entered the final bedroom, we noted the energy was again different from the other rooms. We stood silently in the room and checked and double-checked.

Martin spoke first, "I cannot find anything, can you?" He directed the question at me.

I agreed. I couldn't find anything either.

Suddenly the room became colder and Karen remarked about this. She also said she felt something that was not at all nice was watching her, and she could feel its eyes boring into her.

Karen was right. There was a feeling that eyes were watching from behind—however, we agreed this was an illusion created by the entity to control the environment.

I looked out the window and, in the distance, I could see a hospital. Things were beginning to make sense. We went about clearing and re-energizing the room.

We had now cleared every bedroom, so we went back downstairs to where Paul and Alison's partner Richard sat talking. We worked around them as we checked out the remainder of the house. All felt clear. We still had a lot of work to do as we needed to clear the energy out from underneath the house and move the ley line so that it ran around the building rather than right through it.

In this instance, think of a ley line as a stream of flowing water. Imagine the stream running down from the mountain as clear as crystal and ever in motion. Now think of a stagnant pool of water that has nowhere to go. If it is not replenished by new and vibrant flowing water, it becomes putrid. If there is a factory or a large establishment nearby, such as a hospital, the outlet from the other building runs into the pool. The only thing that gets added is dirt and rubbish. Since hospitals are typically places of upset and misery, and there was one nearby, it would appear that the ley line running underneath the hospital also ran underneath Alison's house. Because there was a node directly under the house, this was adding to the problem as this is the point where the trapped energy will release. When the stagnant energy reaches critical mass it can begin to influence the emotions of those people on or close by it—it can begin to cause ill feelings or arguments amongst the occupants. A being like the thing in Alison's house will flourish in such an environment.

We all mentally worked at pushing the ley line across so that it landed in between the two buildings. We capped the vortex in the front room after first creating an opening for the energy, and then we flushed it out with pure white light.

I asked Richard to please find some rocks or huge pebbles similar to the kind found on beaches, and then to partially bury them in the ground in the area of the ley line. We would then be able to come back and route the ley line across to these stones so the energy could flow via the stones.

Several months after this, I saw Alison and she told me that Richard had collected several stones, which were now partly buried in the ground around the side of the house. The entity thankfully hadn't returned, but her powerful dreams had, and she said the energy in the conservatory didn't feel right.

"What conservatory?" I asked.

"Didn't I show it to you?" she asked. The conservatory was located at the rear of the property off the dining room. It could not be seen from the road and with the curtains drawn, so we did not know of its existence until she told us.

A few days later I returned to Alison's, this time with Linda, Bill, and some students from my group, Sharon and Carol. The gushing energy was still present in the front of the property and all present could feel it.

To our surprise, we found the ley line was still curved around the side of the house channeled between Alison's home and the adjoining property. Along the side of the house were several rocks partly set in the ground.

As we entered the conservatory, we all simultaneously picked up a pool of dark, negative energy that was lying beneath the place. Some of this energy extended under one of the corners of the kitchen but nowhere else. We cleared the ground underneath and extended it out to encompass the whole of the garden. We then gave the ley line a further nudge to ensure it was truly aligned with the stones.

Alison reported her daughters were sleeping so much better and never mentioned the monster. Their son now gladly slept in his old bedroom.

A House in Darkness

By the time Maureen and Pete found me they were really at a breaking point. They lived together with their son Steve in a semi-detached house and were two very peaceful, caring people whose main focus in life was animal rescue. They had lived on the same property for many years and the problems had only started to develop a couple of years ago.

Steve appeared to be the focus of some of these frightening and unnatural events. On several occasions he had been knocked to the floor and suffered physical attacks. Once, in the company of his parents, deep, red scratch marks had suddenly appeared on his back to the extent that blood was drawn. Steve was also tormented in his bedroom. The family rarely used the living room as they found the atmosphere too oppressive. To top it off, the family found themselves continually arguing with one another for no apparent reason.

The property itself was a very nice three-bedroom place built about seventy years ago and set in a small housing complex. It was very fortunate the area had not been over-developed and fields and woods ran along the bottom of the garden.

When we arrived, we checked out the kitchen and it felt normal, but the same could not be said of the living room. As soon as we entered this spacious room I felt the need to duck, as if I were in a room with very low beams on the ceiling. I could also feel the presence of another property, as if the ethereal vibration of a small, low cottage overlay the room and out buildings.

As usual, all the classic signs were there—the house was cold, dark, and dismal. The three light bulbs in the chandelier did little to lighten the room, and a free-standing lamp with two bulbs in it threw out very little light.

After doing a walk around the property we decided we had two problems to deal with—one was in the living room and the other in the bedroom. We had found two entities that had a very angry feel to them.

Lyn, Bill, Paul, and I began by focusing our attention on the living room and we saved the bedroom for last.

In the living room, each and every one of us felt we could almost reach out and touch the walls of the former cottage, so great was its imprint. It was as if the past and present had become intertwined.

Quickly we became aware of a very angry male spirit. He seemed trapped here by some unearthly event and couldn't understand what we were doing in his home. He was very aware of Maureen, Pete, and Steve—more so than they were of him. He saw all three of them as intruders and he had been doing all he could to get them out. And the man was not alone. His wife was also there with him. From the clothing he was wearing it was obvious that he did not belong to this century; he seemed to be of the 1800s. This was a very hard man who, despite any hard work he had done, had lived his life in poverty. He had been a drunk who had tormented his family by beating them on a regular basis. It was this anger and violence that tied him to the astral plane, and somehow his unfortunate family had become entangled in his vibration.

Within moments the spirit world came with its usual skill and perfection and separated out the energetic fields of these two vastly different families. In no time, the former cottage was disentangled and returned to its rightful dimension.

We soon felt this situation was the least of our problems as we sensed there was something far more sinister residing in the house. It was this entity that had kept all the other ethereal occupants of the place captive.

For example, a very sinister, angry, dark energy was lurking in the bedroom. The entity stood about three feet tall and appeared to have the presence of what can only be described as a small, very hairy caveman. This entity did not belong to this world and didn't really want to be here. Its vibration was alien to our plane of existence; the entity was filled with what we saw as rage, but that was normal for him. The being had somehow gotten trapped here. We knew it was dangerous to try to communicate with it directly, but through the intercession of our guides we began to receive information. The entity was as unhappy to be here as this family was to have it in residence, but the fact was, it was trapped and unable to return to its own dimension. In the meantime, while it had been here, it had run amok. Enjoyment was not a concept it understood, but it had begun to receive some gratification from interacting with the family in a negative way—and it had been harvesting their fear and growing fatter in the process.

"This entity belongs in the ground," I said.

"Yes, I know," Bill replied. "And it's not at all happy to be here." He then went on to say the entity was actually furious about being locked in this house.

We then began to pick up that this hairy caveman had lived deep down in the earth amongst the rocks. Lyn remarked that she felt there had been mining done close by and this being was somehow linked to that occupation.

There had been some procedure that had thrown him from his world and trapped him in ours.

Pete readily agreed, stating that at the back of the house there had been a former working pit. A couple of years ago, work had been carried out to fill the pit and cap it. We then knew it had been this disturbance that had catapulted the entity from one world to the other. With the 1800s cottage superimposed over the modern house, a sort of time slip had happened and the two events had been locked together.

The team worked together and we managed to open an appropriate doorway and begin the process of shifting this angry creature back to his own dimension. Kicking and screaming, he was soon returned to his own world.

We now moved through the rest of the house.

In the downstairs bathroom we found two small spirit children hiding up in the corner. These were probably associated with the man in the lounge.

"Has he gone?" they asked Lyn.

When Lyn told the children it was safe, they needed no encouragement, and in a moment they were down and through the silver doorway that had opened for them.

The positive impact on the house was immediate. We could feel the warmth begin to penetrate through the whole of the building and the brightness could clearly be seen, especially in the living room.

A couple of months afterward, I bumped into Maureen and she was full of enthusiasm and couldn't find the words to express the difference our visit had made in their lives. They had always been a fairly peaceful couple that preferred to talk things out rather than argue, but she said by the time we had visited, arguments had become a daily occurrence. This had caused a great strain on the relationship among all three of them, to the point where she and her husband had considered divorce. Now things had thankfully returned to normal and all talk of ending the marriage had ceased. They were back to sitting in the living room, and now the five 100-watt bulbs that had been used to light up the room had been replaced with only one.

Just as a side note to this clearance I must remark that it almost didn't go ahead as I was unable to find the street, even though I knew the area very well. I couldn't call for help as, coincidentally, Pete's phone was turned off despite them expecting me. I, of course, did eventually arrive but thirty minutes late. I knew that somehow the entity had cloaked the entrance to the street from me so I would hopefully go away.

Conclusion

Over a period of time these encounters and experiences changed my outlook on life and the way I perceived the world to be. I discovered that a whole other dimension existed and sometimes that dimension and the earth plane collided, and those collisions took place either because of faults in the etheric net, or due to the misuse of the Ouija board or some other method of spirit communication. Once the doorway between the dimensions is opened, it is often very nearly impossible to close it. The entities that enter the earth plane, unfortunately, are not of the beneficent kind, but rather come in to wreak havoc. These beings are not ghosts or shadow forms from the past—they are evil entities capable of thinking and planning their moves with the aim of creating terror and fear. This fear is what they harvest and use to make themselves stronger. The human victims of these entities find themselves being tormented by these powerful forces. Most of the time these victims find the nightmare only ends when someone like me or my colleagues are called in to help.

In contrast, I have also learned that every dark force has a light force in the form of angels, guides, and light warriors who surround the world with goodness and are ready and willing to defeat the darkness. The way to access these defenders of the defenseless is quite simple: believe in their presence and request their assistance.

I've also learned of the resiliency of human beings and their innate capacity to withstand horrible onslaughts from negative entities without giving in. The mind of mortal man can shut out situations in order to protect itself from the reality of a nightmarish mental or psychic attack.

There is no doubt in my mind that stories such as those written here will continue as long as ghosts and demons walk the earth.

I would like to leave you with a prayer of protection that I use every day: "I call upon these spirits present to protect the doorway to my soul. Protect me from deception and dark forces and only allow spirits that come with Love, Light, Truth, and Happiness to communicate with me in any way, shape, or form. Amen."